D1726229

Ansgar Walk • Kenojuak

Herrn Eckard Zimmermann
in alter Verbundenheit
nun auch die englische
Fassung –
mit allen guten Wünschen
von
Ansgar & Ulrike Walk
18. 10. 2000

Ansgar Walk

Kenojuak

The life story of an
Inuit artist

Penumbra Press

Original German Edition © Pendragon Verlag, Bielefeld 1998

Translation from German origin: Timothy B. Spence

CANADIAN CATALOGUING IN PUBLICATION DATA

Walk, Ansgar
       Kenojuak : an Inuit artist's life story

Includes bibliographical references.
ISBN 0-921254-95-4

   1. Kenojuak, 1927-   2. Inuit artists—Canada—Biography.
3. Cape Dorset (Nunavut)—Social conditions.   I. Title

N6549.K454W34   1999   709'.2   C99-901348-3

Contents

Part II
In hospital

Part III
Back in camps

Part IV
In the settlement

Annex

Sikusiilaq:
Cape Dorset at open waters

This is the story of an important Inuit artist. It tells how the people on the southwest coast of Baffin Island lived a life full of drama and privations in two different 'worlds' – their traditional Inuit culture and, increasingly, the 20th-century western culture.

For thousands of years, humans have settled along the southwest coast of Baffin Island and its archipelago of islands in the Hudson Strait, attracted by the good hunting grounds. Even in the coldest of winters, the currents in the Hudson Strait prevent the sea from freezing over here and there; as a result extensive polynia are formed – areas of open water in which sea mammals can sojourn. Sikusiilaq, 'where the water does not freeze,' is the name given to this area by the Inuit, who call themselves Sikusiilarmiut, 'people of Sikusiilaq.'

The first European to come here was probably Luke Foxe. He explored the Hudson Strait in the year 1631 and gave one of the many coastal islands jutting into the Strait the name Cape Dorset – in honour of his master, Edward Sackville, Earl of Dorset. Among the Inuit, however, the island and the settlement that later arose here bear the name Kinngait, after the high mountain that dominates it. The second half of the last century saw whalers, mainly Scots and North Americans, come in growing numbers to the southwest coast of Baffin Island. In 1913, the Hudson's Bay Company established an outpost here, and the first *qallunaat* (white men) to settle in Cape Dorset soon followed. This gave a powerful boost to the fur trade with the hunters and trappers that lived in numerous camps along the coast. A decade later, the search for an extinct paleo-Eskimo culture conducted by Diamond Jenness, the anthropologist, was crowned with success, and Cape Dorset lent its name to an entire culture – Dorset culture.

In 1927, Kenojuak was born in one of the nearby Inuit camps. Many details of her life reflect the radical upheavals and changes that have since occurred in Canada's Arctic North. Apart from several years in a lung clinic in Quebec, she spent the first half of her life in the traditional manner – 'on the land' – in camps along the Hudson Strait coastline, before moving permanently to the settlement at the foot of Kinngait mountain.

The whalers were accompanied by the first Anglican missionaries to this part of the country, bringing Christianity to the Inuit. Yet it was not until 1938-39 that the first church building was established in Cape Dorset, by Roman Catholic Missionary Oblates. Their efforts met with little missionary success in the ensuing period, however. The Inuit, mostly adherents of Anglican theology, built their own church in the settlement in 1953 (Pootoogook's Church). The Catholic church remained empty for a long time thereafter, and was finally abandoned in 1960.

After the Second World War, the Arctic North was the object of growing strategic interest. At that time, the majority of the Inuit were still living the whole year round in their camps outside the communities and would come to the settlements only once or twice a year to trade at the Hudson's Bay stores what hunting had yielded them (mainly fox fur). They would return with everyday needs, such as hunting weapons, ammunition, sugar, salt, tea, coffee and fabrics.

In the early 1950s, this way of life was to undergo fundamental change; the Canadian government took the indigenous population of this region under its wing – with varying degrees of success. Gradually but progressively, utilities and the concomitant infrastructure were created on Baffin Island.

In 1950, one of the first schools in the Eastern Arctic was established in Cape Dorset, as was a small nursing station. For all the progressiveness of such facilities from our own present-day viewpoint, the Inuit were confronted by a radical and incisive process that would last more than a decade and transform their entire nomadic way of life. They would be almost totally sedentary, moving, voluntarily in most cases, from camps to settlements. Epidemics and starvation were frequent causes as well, however. In 1970, only one permanent camp remained in Sikusiilaq; a year later, it, too, was abandoned.

Life in a wooden house supplied with water, electricity and heat superseded their former life in *qarmaqs* (sod houses), igloos or tents made from skins and canvas. The Inuit became consumers whose livelihood consisted only partially of fishing, hunting and trapping. Essentially, however, they saw themselves compelled to produce handicrafts or accept wage labour (in 'services'), in order to obtain money – something on which they are now dependent in contrast to the past. Many Inuit have to be subsidized with social welfare benefits as well, and it is no rarity for state welfare to be the one and only source of income. Needs are now met with food and consumer goods from the South, as opposed to their former self-sufficiency through hunting. Camp life is now a thing of the past, lost forever. The fact that many still go hunting and fishing with great keenness any time they get the chance, and that, for most Inuit, frequent stays in a tent or cabin on the land are now a substitute for camp life, does not detract from the fundamental change their lifestyle has undergone.

A system of local government and a regiment of the Royal Canadian Mounted Police (RCMP) were established in 1962 and 1965, respectively. In the eyes of the Inuit, these were unusual and therefore 'suspect' administrative centres, run along the lines of an industrialized state by non-indigenous Canadian civil servants. Understandably, adapting to such extraneous rule has been no easy matter for the Inuit. Many, especially the elders who never learned the English language and who are able to express themselves in Inuktitut only, have still not adapted fully to these changes. Adjustment to different conditions of life was easiest for young people, of course. The younger generations have gained many new opportunities in recent decades, but these have also involved hardship and difficulties of various kinds. To mention just one example: the traditional system of 'learning from one's parents,' in which reading or writing had no place, gave way to compulsory schooling. In the early days, this often meant children were separated from their parents because not all settlements had their own school.

The creation of Inuit co-operatives played a paramount role in this context. Here, people learned to organize value-added activities and to manage by themselves again. After establishing such a co-operative in Cape Dorset in the late 1950s, people there succeeded in exemplary fashion not only in organizing and selling their art products profitably, but also in combining business-mindedness with traditional activities and values.

I
Life in camps

Ikirasak and Pujjunnaq:
Early childhood and the violent death of her father

Kenojuak, or Qinnuajuak to be more phonetically precise, first saw the light of this world in 1927, in Camp Ikirasak. The camp, totally deserted today, was situated on the southern coast of Baffin Island, about 80 km to the east of Cape Dorset at the southeast corner of Andrew Gordon Bay – looking out to Hudson Strait. Ikirasak means 'Strait.'

In those days, the Inuit mainly lived in small groups comprising a number of different families, in camps located as close as possible to the coast. These groups were held together by kinship ties in most cases and were led by a dominant personality, the camp leader. Such a leader was usually someone with a powerful will and determination and skilled in hunting; in many cases, he possessed a distinctive charisma.

Kenojuak was born into the extended family of a widely recognized shaman, or *angakkuq*. Her father, Usuaqjuk, was a son of Alariaq, a shaman; her mother was called Silaqqi. October 3, 1927 is registered as her date of birth, but the specific date is rather indefinite. Such information was needed for official purposes only, for example to obtain a passport. Kenojuak, in any case, tells us that she was born shortly after a big winter feast, probably Christmas. She concludes that she was born in early 1927 – 'in an igloo,' she adds with obvious pride. Like all Inuit, she does not make a song and dance about birthdays and has rarely wasted a thought on the fact that she has just turned seventy.

There is much about the hour of my birth that has remained in my memory and that I can tell you about. For example, I can well remember how I tried to get outside to the light – because I could see this light well. But there was something that stopped me when I wanted to push myself forward, and so I withdrew again and again. But then I finally managed to get out into the open. It was very bright and cold there. First I saw two large hills on the left and on the right – these were the thighs of my mother, and between them a valley into which I came. I saw giant people before me, and their enormous hands picked me up. I still know exactly how I began to cry when they lifted me up. I wanted to flee but couldn't. Then I must have fallen asleep again because I can only remember up to there.

Astonished and somewhat disbelieving, we ask her whether these details are more likely to be gleaned from the narrations of others. But Kenojuak, supported by our interpreter, Jeannie Manning, a grand-daughter of Peter Pitseolak, the well-known camp leader, replied, "No, no, there's nothing unusual about that, and there's no need for you to be so surprised. There are lots of people here in the settlement who, just like myself, can remember many things about their birth."

Peter Pitseolak, for one, describes details of his birth in his recollections, emphasizing that, although everything appears as if in a dream, he is recounting a true experience.[1]

Kenojuak's ancestors originated from the northern part of Quebec. Her father, Usuaqjuk, was born near Ivujivik in the early years of the century. Her mother Silaqqi was born around 1902 on Avilik, the Ottawa Islands southwest of the

Puvirnituk (formerly Povungnituk) settlement. They probably married around or shortly after 1920.

In the years following the turn of the century, the scarcity of animals to hunt led to increasingly severe starvation among the Inuit. In the worst year of all, 1911, they were finally compelled to go in search of new hunting grounds. Word had got around that there were still some areas with plenty of wild animals on the other side of the Hudson Strait, on Baffin Island. It was a welcome coincidence that a Scottish whaling ship, the *Active*, had been in Arctic waters since the turn of the century hunting for sea mammals and searching for minerals, and was spending much of its time in the Hudson Strait between northern Quebec and the south coast of Baffin. Its captain, Alexander Murray jr., was glad to take Inuit people on board as temporary workers, paying for their services with hunting rifles and other goods, and not least by transporting them to distant camps. The Inuit men were employed to catch whale, seal and walrus, while the women were responsible for processing the catch to obtain skins and oil.

Many Inuit from northern Quebec took this as an opportunity to move across the Hudson Strait to the southern part of Baffin Island, to Sikusiilaq and the Lake Harbour region, so that they could take advantage of the better conditions for survival these areas seemed to offer. Kimmirut, in particular, which was still called Lake Harbour at that time, exerted a certain attraction on the Inuit. The owner of the *Active*, the Tay Whale Fishing Company from Dundee in Scotland under the direction of Robert Kinness, had set up a trading post there a few years previously and operated on the site of today's community a mica and graphite mine where the Inuit could work for money. In the wake of these changes, an Anglican missionary station was established here in 1909, headed by one Reverend Archibald Fleming, a later bishop. In 1911, the Hudson's Bay

Company set up their first fur trading post and their district headquarters for Baffin Island.

Both sets of Kenojuak's grandparents were among those who left northern Quebec aboard the *Active*, taking most of their family with them to the south coast of Baffin Island.

Conditions there were anything but paradisiacal, as can be seen from the descriptions by Peter Pitseolak.[2] At that time, he and his brother, Pootoogook, were living with their families in Camp Ulimavik, near Markham Bay, about 130 kilometres northwest of Kimmirut. They were the only residents of the camp at first and were lucky to find sufficient animals to kill, mainly caribou and seal. But it was not long before people between Cape Dorset and Kimmirut got word that there was food to be had in the area around Ulimavik. In any case, more and more people who could not find enough to eat elsewhere came here to settle.

Peter Pitseolak adds that the people of Akudnik, for example – which is the stretch of land to the west of Kimmirut – were actually on the verge of starvation all the time although they did not wish to admit this and spurned any form of stockpiling. Only fresh meat was to their taste, quite obviously. In fact, the number of animals was rarely enough to meet their food requirements, and so the people in that area had to rely again and again on support from the Hudson's Bay Company.

Things were quite different with the Sikusiilarmiut, the camp dwellers around Cape Dorset. They considered themselves, and rightly so, to be more cunning and more intelligent than the Inuit living near Kimmirut and on the islands. It was a habit of theirs to save a portion of their hunting yield as a meat reserve and had to tolerate being mocked for this by the people of Akudnik, who would say, "Oh, the people of Sikusiilaq, they eat rotten meat...."

There is an Inuktitut word for the season of extreme starvation – *akunnaaqi*, which literally means 'between two states.' They are referring here to the period between winter and summer, in which hunting rarely meets with success. In the words of Peter Pitseolak:[3]

Then the snow on the land is soft and the sleds stick. It was not much use going after the animals – you couldn't catch them. On the ice you could sink and if you used the kayak on the open water sharp ice pieces could dig in and make holes. Then the currents in the water are strong and at this time the young seals can run away quickly. We would go after the seaweeds and dulse and eat them with the aged-blubber dip. It was nutritious – we weren't weak – but you couldn't eat too much of it; you'd get a stomach ache, a bad case of indigestion.

When the men wanted to go hunting very badly they would throw into the ice a naked baby bird or a baby lemming that still had no fur and hope for the north wind to scare away the ice. This was the old, old custom. It worked – sometimes.... When I was growing up I also heard that when the weather was very, very bad in the summertime and the waters were rough for many days, the men would go looking for a raven. They would hope for a raven that was very, very fat … a raven with a lot of fat in the stomach. That was the best. They took the fat and pounded it with a rock. Then they threw the fat into the sea and hoped for calm waters. Sometimes it worked, sometimes it didn't.

The situation in Sikusiilaq was different. Because the water there remained open, there was less drift ice, and the hunters could put out their *kayaks* even in deep winter and hunt seal or walrus. The starving people in the Kimmirut area kept their eyes on the ice floes, however. If they had black marks, this indicated that someone had killed a walrus, and they would then travel around on their sleds until they had found the successful hunters.

It is obvious that starvation used to drive people to extreme behaviour, even to cannibalism. Peter Pitseolak knows of such cases from hearsay.[4]

In my life I have never come across a real starvation – I know of only two people who died from starvation. But there's a place over the hill from Frobisher Bay where before I was born people died from hunger after eating each other. They started from Markham Bay but they ran into spring. They were travelling by dog team when the snow melted and they had to walk across. Just recently somebody found an old *kayak* that had belonged to them at the place where they died. They starved around Frobisher Bay. I don't know how many there were but I've heard they were many.

Sometimes starving people kill a person to eat. When they had to do this they always picked a boss. The boss selected was not necessarily the smartest person but he'd be a boss of the killings. He'd tell them who to kill. It didn't matter who you were when the man in charge of the killings said, "I want that person." He had to be fat – to be a good candidate to be eaten. The boss would tell the people to kill whoever he thought would be the best to eat. These people killed their camp boss first. They came to life for a while on him. Then they started to starve again. Two women were the only survivors; they did not kill each other – maybe because they were not bosses. They started to walk when there was no one left to eat. One of them had a little girl – she was not a baby but they carried her to keep her warm. As they walked they gave her some of the human meat so she would not starve. They walked down to the bay and there people found them. They weren't moving at all.

They couldn't go on. They were just sitting there on the tails of their 'amoutik' – their parkas. When people found them their faces were so skinny they looked as if they were smiling.

Inuit people say if a person has eaten a human being his mouth is always dark. I have often asked Aggeok, who knew the baby who was carried and survived, "Was her mouth dark?" Aggeok always says, "I am sure it was dark."

In the year 1929, almost two decades after moving to the south coast of Baffin Island, most of Alariaq's family seized on the plan to leave Ikirasak and visit some relatives who had remained in northern Quebec, near Ivujivik, and perhaps to return for good to their traditional homeland.

About the same time, Peter Pitseolak took his family from Tujak (Nottingham Island), where he had found well-paid work on a Canadian Air Force base a year previously, to live with his elder brother, Pootoogook. The latter had just taken over Camp Ikirasak after it was abandoned by Alariaq, and so the Inuit people of Cape Dorset have called Ikirasak 'Pootoogook's camp' ever since.

Kenojuak was just over two years of age when her grandfather Alariaq crossed the Hudson Strait together with his family, and she can still recall some fragments of the voyage. Alariaq owned a small wooden Peterhead boat, the *Nanukudluk*, and it was in this boat that they crossed the Hudson Strait to the south. Kenojuak spent the crossing lying on the bottom of a canoe that had been strapped aboard and watched attentively what her parents and the other relatives were doing. They had their sled dogs on board as well, which caused a few problems. When the dogs had to do their business, they were tied up and held over the railings by their rear end with their tails until the job was done.

While the boat was approaching Qiqiqtarjuaq Inlet, which is near Ivujivik and also called Anauvirlik, Kenojuak especially was struck by the flock of startled black guillemots rising from the cliffs. Nevertheless, she kept falling asleep again in the canoe.

The family split up when they reached the coast of Qiqiqtarjuaq Inlet. Alariaq and his wife stayed here with their new-born son, Nutahaluk, while the others travelled onwards to Pujjunnaq, which is the Inuit name for Mansel Island. They intended to stay there for a while in a rather large camp and go hunting.

Kenojuak remembers that, when they were living on the island, there was a very charming man and much respected hunter who played an eminent role in the life of the community. His name was Qalingo. He had at that time been employed by a white trader, with responsibility for handling the fur trade business with the indigenous population. His sister Quaraq was related to Kenojuak's grandmother Quitsaq, and took charge of the little girl the second she arrived, carrying her around in her *amautiq* everywhere she went even though the little girl had been able to walk for some time. An unusually close relationship soon developed between the two. Kenojuak, her eyes radiating joy, told us that she had visited Quaraq Ainalik, now in a ripe old age, in Ivujivik recently.

On Pujjunnaq, Kenojuak also felt increasingly drawn to her father. She remembers him as a friendly, well-meaning man, and an excellent hunter. When sharing out the kill, he was often particularly generous towards those Inuit people who had not been as successful on the hunt as he, and this made a deep impression on her. When her brother Adamie, one year younger than herself, grew up to become a man, she recognized the amazing likeness he bore to his father in this respect.

In 1930, in the summer after their arrival on Pujjunnaq, fate struck the small group a first, terrible blow. One exceedingly dark night with little visibility, a terrible storm suddenly arose in the Hudson Strait. Kenojuak's uncle Enoyuk, her father's younger brother, was still out on the water with his wife, children and other Inuit, in a wooden boat that was not very seaworthy. They were caught completely by surprise. They did everything in their power to escape the tempestuous waves and reach land, but in vain. The boat was flung against the cliffs jutting out from the land, and all in the boat drowned before the eyes of those waiting on the shore. Kenojuak experienced the children's horrific drowning as if she herself were afflicted by this fate; these children had been very dear to her. Whenever talk turns to that unforgettable night, she can still see her weeping parents in her mind's eye.

Kenojuak's father was obviously a feared man among the Inuit on Pujjunnaq and little loved despite his generous nature. This may be attributable to the fact that, in the years prior to his departure from northern Quebec, Usuaqjuk's father Alariaq had been an important *angakkuq* (shaman) who possessed much greater knowledge than normal mortals, and that people thought his son would have such extraordinary powers as well. Although Alariaq had ceased his activities as a shaman many years before, due to the influence of Reverend Peck, an Anglican missionary, the Inuit did not change their view of him. For them, Alariaq would always be a real *angakkuq*. For example, Alariaq could predict certain events; indeed he himself was often part of supernatural happenings. From all that we know about him, he never used his knowledge to harm others; instead, he knew how to help other people when they were having problems. He was known to turn himself into the spirit of a walrus and undertake perilous journeys to the goddess of the sea mammals in the depths of the sea in order to support his friends in their search for food. It is also said of

Alariaq that he had the power to make himself invisible, to be eaten by animals and to heal deadly harpoon wounds.

Alariaq himself once told Peter Pitseolak a story about his shamanic powers. One evening Alariaq, Peter Pitseolak's cousin Mapaluk and a third man were out hunting. Suddenly they saw a caribou – an unusually large animal. They grabbed their rifles, each man wanting to be the first to shoot the beast. But Alariaq smiled at them and said that he wanted to test his powers and kill the caribou with his spirit alone. Alariaq knew, of course, that shamans are able to kill other people with their spiritual powers. Some shamans were, therefore, very dangerous to their fellow human beings. But Alariaq was a good shaman, and so he wanted to try out his powers of killing with his spirit on an animal. The three men sat and waited. The caribou came closer and closer, until it was hidden by a hill. No sooner had the caribou disappeared behind it Alariaq went to the other side of the hill to face the animal. For minutes he did not speak a word. Then he said to his two companions, "The caribou is dead. You can go to it now." The two men then saw the animal lying on the ground – well and truly dead. Mapaluk was most surprised, and of course he told everybody of this experience. Alariaq told the two men accompanying him that they could take the skin and divide it among themselves. He wanted no part for himself, otherwise he might die. They took the skin, but the entrails, the intestines, the lungs, everything, had turned to blood. For that reason, they decided to leave the meat as well.[5]

Alariaq also told Peter Pitseolak that he had two spirits working for him – a dog and a spirit by the name of Mikeajuk, which means 'fur in the mouth.' Mikeajuk was a human being. He had no teeth but was covered in fur everywhere, even inside his mouth. When Peter Pitseolak asked him why he also had fur inside his mouth, Alariaq said briefly and concisely to him: "That was like that, because he was Mikeajuk [fur in the mouth]."

Alariaq also told about his journeys to the bottom of the sea. Peter Pitseolak notes, with the frequent repetitions common among Inuit, that:

> Whenever people in the camp were hungry he'd go underwater to reach the beautiful lady at the bottom of the sea and find food. When the shaman made this journey he'd have to sing songs to his spirit.
>
> The path to the bottom of the sea was very dangerous with smooth and very slippery ice. The reason the shaman went was to bring the animals close to where the hunters were. Along the journey there were many animals. And all around the beautiful lady the animals were thick as flies. They looked like a mass of insects clustered together. This lady had so many animals – the usual animals, most of them food animals, the sea animals and, yes, the tuktu [caribou], too. All kinds of animals. She was the goddess of the animals. After Alariak had made this journey, the men would go out hunting and they would find food. Alariak didn't actually get the food from the lady.

Peter Pitseolak is not sure whether 'the beautiful lady' is the same as Talilayuk, also known throughout the North as Sedna, but he believes so. His brother, Pootoogook, may have seen Talilayuk once from a distance – he thought he was seeing a seal at first, but when the being began swinging its arms he knew it was not a seal.

When we asked her what she herself knows about her grandfather, Alariaq, Kenojuak broke out into amused laughter and replied, "He was much too heavy. He was a fat man – and a good man." Occasionally he would pretend to close his eyes in order to concentrate his thoughts or to meditate; but she was a sharp observer and says, "I am quite sure he was only sleeping." He was doubtlessly an important personality with unusual charisma.

Jeannie, our interpreter, adds a little story to what has been said so far. Her grandfather, Peter Pitseolak, was once very ill and close to death because an 'evil' shaman wished him ill. However, the 'good' shaman, Alariaq, then pitted himself against the 'evil' shaman, repelled it and healed her grandfather. One should mention here that Peter Pitseolak refers, in his recollections, to his own grandfather, Etidlooie, always warning against believing in shamans or spirits. Relating to himself he writes:

> Before I was born there were so many shamans. They had their helpers of course. They could make helpers from any kind of animal, from worms, bugs and the spirits of dead people.... When I was born there were not obvious shamans – Okhamuk [lit. 'who speaks so well;' the reference is to the Reverend Edmund J. Peck] had told them to repent – but they were still sneaking around behind Okhamuk's back. Aggeok's grandmother[6] used to fly in the air; Parr's mother[7] used to jump on a harpoon to fly.... I've known so many shamans and know so many stories. I can imitate shamans. I've even got photographs of shamans. But I don't like shamans. Even the good shamans belonged to the devil. [As a child] I've heard many times of the things they could do but since I've been old enough to understand things, I've never seen real shaman work.[8]

Kenojuak states that she has never come into direct contact with traditional Inuit shamanism at all. Even the oldest members of the community, such as Simeonie Quppapik, have no personal experience of shamanism as far as they know. In their childhood days, Christianity had obviously gained a firm foothold. Alariaq, for his part, was no longer an active *angakkuq*, and even participated actively in services now and then. He prayed frequently and also taught Kenojuak to pray and to believe in Jesus Christ. Most importantly, she tells us, he taught her 'not to hate other people.'

The winter of 1930-31 was a deeply oppressive in every respect. In the camp on Pujjunnaq there was much talk about the progressive decline in the prices paid for animal skins. The ground was prepared for tensions in everyday life. Kenojuak is not sure whether her father had occasionally uttered threats to other hunters. It seems quite likely because she remembers him as a vehement and often very impulsive man, perhaps even hot-tempered. In any case, some of the men in the camp were apparently of the opinion that Usuaqjuk's presence was fanning the flames of strife. Dramatic events unfolded.

It must have been a terrible time for Silaqqi. Kenojuak tells us what happened from the perspective of a child too young to comprehend the deeper roots, and from accounts of events that she heard later. "My mother was overcome by deep fear; at times she thought Usuaqjuk was behaving as if he had lost all his senses."

In Cape Dorset, however, we heard reports that shed a different light on the looming disaster and Usuaqjuk's fate. Many years previously, in his capacity as camp leader, Alariaq is supposed to have condemned a man to death in accordance with traditional Inuit laws because the latter had severely mistreated his family and could no longer be tolerated in the camp. Alariaq chose his own son, Usuaqjuk, to execute judgement, with the result that he now had a fellow human being's death on his hands.

Such events may seem incomprehensible to us, in any case inhuman. However, before passing judgement one should reflect that the sense of justice among the Inuit at that time was centred, of necessity, on maintaining harmony and stability. This was the only way to ensure the survival of the group as a whole. Anyone who became too quarrelsome, lost his temper, persistently disturbed family life or who failed to respect the property of other group members was a threat to the entire community. In such a case, the camp leader was compelled to re-establish order. Now and then, members of the camp would take the 'solution to the problem' into their own hands, either through individual initiative or group pressure. Unfortunately, an execution did not put an end to matters in most cases then, and further killings were frequently the outcome of ensuing family feuds.

In any case, Usuaqjuk's past had also become common knowledge on Pujjunnaq and conferred on him an exceptional status. Since he had inherited his father's charismatic aura and was a good hunter as well, there were more than a few men in the camp who felt inferior to him in many respects. Feelings of envy mounted against the stranger who had come here from the Baffin region.

Whatever may have led to the tragedy, there is a dreadful winter's day burned deep and irrevocably into Kenojuak's memory. In the morning, Usuaqjuk was getting ready to leave for the hunt and all of a sudden became involved in a loud argument with another man. Afterwards, he returned to his igloo and threw himself onto the sleeping platform where the children were cuddled in their warm skins. In this hour, he must already have suspected what was in store for him, and was probably beginning to accept his inevitable fate. Because he behaved differently than otherwise – flailing wildly with his fists, throwing himself from one side to the other. Now and then he wept bitterly, then he would talk with his children, friendly and apparently calm. Silaqqi and Qalingo tried to placate him – to no avail.

All of a sudden he got up and left the igloo. Several shots fell. Silaqqi burst outside, the children following. Little Kenojuak saw her father lying in a pool of blood that was slowly seeping into the snow; he did not stir. She knew then that his life had come to an end.

Three men had been waiting outside to murder Usuaqjuk. When the deed was done, they began to tie rocks to his neck, his wrists and his ankles, before letting the weighted body drop down into the sea. Everything he owned they flung after him. They even shot a few of his dogs; the others got away and never dared to come near the camp again.

Kenojuak's words to us: "My father was obviously not keeping to the rules of conduct in our camp. So it was decided he should die." Yet if the real motive for the murder was nothing but envy, as other Inuit people describe, then Kenojuak's mother must have faced a terrible dilemma. In order to protect the rest of her family against any further calamities, she could not permit herself to show any loyalty to her dead husband. Instead, she had to withhold the true circumstances from her children.

Sapujjuaq and Igalaalik: Girlhood years

The winter weeks ahead were to be exceptionally hard on Silaqqi and her children. At every step and turn they sensed the spurning, almost hostile attitude towards them on the part of many camp-dwellers. Besides that, having lost the family breadwinner, they were now exposed to the constant and agonising threat of starvation; luckily, Qalingo and the one or other resident of the camp would let them have some food from their reserves whenever they were able to do so. The fact that Silaqqi was pregnant at the time of her husband's death did not make matters any easier. And yet, burdened by increasing anxiety and plagued by unrelenting feelings of shame and disgrace following the murder of her husband, she succeeded in rising above herself and did not lose heart in the slightest. Spring had yet to arrive when she gave birth to her fourth child, a boy. She named him Attatsi.

The days gradually grew longer, warmth spread over the land, and the ice withdrew from the coast. This was the very time for which Silaqqi had been waiting because her intention was to leave Pujjunnaq with her children as soon as possible. She wanted never again to set foot in this place of horror and shame. Qalingo helped her when it was time for their departure and took them away in his boat. The crossing to Ivujivik was short, and the little group soon arrived at the nearby Kagisualaak trading post (Cape Wolstenholme) operated by the Hudson's Bay Company. Silaqqi waited impatiently for the arrival of the supply ship that usually came only once each summer, in August, also carrying passengers. It was on this ship that she now wanted to travel with her children to

Cape Dorset – to the south coast of Baffin Island on the other side of the Hudson Strait, the place she had left so expectantly two years previously and to which she was now returning, deeply disappointed and distressed.

Her long wait was rewarded when the *Nascopie*, a ship sailing under the Hudson's Bay Company flag, finally dropped anchor at the trading post. The ship's officers made some inquiries about Usuaqjuk's murderers, but the latter had disappeared on Pujjunnaq. The subsequent search was unsuccessful, and the three men involved in the murder were never prosecuted. The *Nascopie*, however, departed for Cape Dorset.

When Dorset Island and the striking silhouette of Eegatuak Hill finally appeared over the horizon, the new arrivals felt relief that Pujjunnaq and the connected dreadful events were now put behind them once and for all. Full of hope, but also with apprehension, they looked forward to being welcomed by their relatives and friends.

It was not long before the ship's anchors were lowered at the mooring point at Cape Dorset. Kenojuak can remember to this day how, when she was being rowed to shore, she initially felt about joining a group of complete strangers again. But then came a big hug from her aunt Tayaraq, her father's elder sister and the one who did not go with them to northern Quebec at the time. Tears ran down Kenojuak's cheeks, and Tayaraq and Silaqqi cried with her. What was quite unusual for this little girl, Kenojuak emphasizes, was that nobody treated her badly even though she was so young and without any form of paternal protection – what must she have been through previously!

In view of the burden involved in bringing up and feeding an extra child, Silaqqi agreed immediately after their arrival to have Attatsi, her baby boy, adopted.

Adoptions – especially within the extended family – are commonplace among the Inuit even to this day, for example when a family or a single mother is unable to care properly for a child. Peter Pitseolak has mentioned some of the reasons for adoption, but in the meantime these only partially apply: "People adopt babies because they privately think, 'When I grow old there will be no one to be with me, to help me around; no one to hunt and bring in the food; no one to do the sewing.' But adopted children are not servants; sometimes they are even more loved than a natural child." [9]

Silaqqi's brothers, Tikituk and Niviaqsi, had walked with a friend of theirs, Etidlooie, from Camp Sapujjuaq to the pier at Cape Dorset in order to fetch the travellers. Their arrival coincided with an official census of the Inuit people being conducted by the Canadian government, so they, too, were recorded. A few days later, the whole group set out across the tundra for the camp. Etidlooie carried Kenojuak, then four years of age, on his back. She remembers making herself comfortable on his backpack and how she kept falling asleep during their hike; but when they stopped to rest, she played with the others.

In the gentle light of an early summer morning, the hikers reached a camp – Sapujjuaq – situated near a river and comprising several tents. Silaqqi's mother, Quitsaq, bade them welcome before the newcomers were allocated their tents. Silaqqi shared a tent with her uncle Tagatuk. Kenojuak and her brother Adamie, however, were allowed to live with their grandmother.

At first, Kenojuak expected having to live again in a new camp with total strangers; she knew no differently, after all. But she soon realized that she had now found a new place to live, here with relatives, and for many years Sapujjuaq was a real home where she could grow up sheltered by her family.

Kenojuak

View from the airstrip at Cape Dorset

Evening over Cape Dorset

Camp Iqalurajuk at Andrew Gordon Bay (cabin and tent)

Iqalurajuk: jigging through the ice on a lake near the camp

Jigging through ice more than two metres thick
to catch Arctic char the length of one's arm

Pressed ice before Camp Iqalurajuk

A morning scene at the cabin in Camp Iqalurajuk

Andrew Gordon Bay, near Camp Ikirasak

Ikirasak, where Kenojuak and her brother Adamie were born

Ikirasak: in front of an old cabin

Ikirasak: the remains of an old *qarmaq*

Inuksuit (stone figures) on a small island before Alareak Island

The grave of Jaku Mamirajak

Itilliaqjuk, Aoudla Pee's former camp

Saatturittuq, the camp of Qaqaq and Mayoreak Ashoona

Camp Sapujjuaq – 'like a fish weir'– was known for its excellent fishing grounds and, therefore, was a magnet for many families. Back in the past, their ancestors had built weirs here from rocks in order to catch fish, and an artificial lake was created as a result. During the seasonal migration of fish, the Inuit waded eagerly into the ice-cold water, using their three-pronged fishing spears to catch huge Arctic chars, some the length of one's arm.

Preserving fish was also well organized in Sapujjuaq. Fish caught for consumption by people were mostly prepared by the women of the camp as stocks for the winter months – gutted, sliced in half, incised in a grid pattern and dried in the air. If used to feed the sled dogs, the fish were not gutted, but kept as they were in 'caches' (stone cairns).

During the cold seasons, a *qarmaq* (sod house) was the usual form of shelter. Although Kenojuak often lived in an igloo (snow house) in winter, especially when travelling, she preferred to live in a *qarmaq* whenever possible. To build one involves making a hollow in the ground and constructing a wood frame to support a roof big enough for the one-room family dwelling. Shortly before the first snowfall, a canvas was stretched over the frame. Beforehand, the women and children would have gathered dry moss in the tundra, which was now spread over the canvas. A second canvas was then laid over the moss layer and fastened to the frame. Winter snow, cut by the men into blocks with their long snow knives, provided additional protection against the elements. Of course, the outer cladding was susceptible to weather conditions and, now and then, would even be gnawed at by wolves and foxes. Since canvas was relatively expensive and sometimes difficult to obtain, the women had to repair it again and again with fingers numb from the icy cold and biting winds. Inside, the *qarmaqs* provided warmth and cosiness from the flame of a *qulliq*, a stone lamp equipped with a moss wick and fuelled by seal oil. A slightly elevated sleeping place covered with caribou skins took up the rear section of the *qarmaq*.

On warm summer days, people left their *qarmaqs* and lived in easily transportable canvas tents; in those days, these were still sewn by the Inuit women themselves. The tents were then taken from camp to camp. In early August, when the first signs of fall appeared, the *qarmaqs* were prepared once again as shelter during the cold months of the year. The frameworks were usually in as intact a condition as they had been left; all that had to be done was to cover them with canvas again.

Quitsaq, Kenojuak's grandmother, had everything she needed despite her advanced years and poor sight; her sons and other relatives took care of her, as was customary among the Inuit at that time. In her calm way marked by the wisdom of old age, she would teach her granddaughter skills that would prove exceedingly helpful in future.

As Kenojuak tells us in this connection, it was common practice for young girls in the camps to do handicrafts and to dream up new designs all the time. Under the guidance of her grandmother, she began at the age of about ten years to produce such work. A young girl, she learned how to sew waterproof seams with caribou sinews, for example, no easy task for such small and inexperienced hands. She was also allowed to make small repairs on skins being prepared for sale to the Hudson's Bay Company. When she had gained enough experience to do needlework and people had confidence in her work, she was permitted to sew together remnants of animal skins. However, there was one skill that she did not acquire completely until she was married – scraping seal fat from skin using an *ulu*, a semicircular woman's knife with handle. That was because she was left-handed.

In those days, being left-handed was obviously embarrassing for the Inuit. To us, at least, Kenojuak admits that when she was a young girl she found this characteristic of hers to be very unpleasant. For example, when she was eating with other people, she did not want to use an *ulu* to cut off a piece of meat because she would have to use her left hand. She probably inherited her left-handedness from her grandfather, Alariaq. He himself had to go through a lot because of this and tried all manner of tricks to wean his granddaughter off using her left hand. Sometimes he would tie the end of her sleeve, but she had no trouble liberating her left arm again. "Perhaps my age is to blame for the fact that I no longer find it embarrassing to be left-handed. But it was hard for me for a long time," she tells us.

Her childhood and youth in Camp Sapujjuaq were untroubled years on the whole, and Kenojuak gladly remembers the many little adventures she had there. With visible enjoyment and a sparkle in her eye, she tells us, for example, about her eager attempts to track small birds and animals in order to catch them; she was so taken by their beauty and wanted to view them at close quarters.

There was no shortage of children's toys. Her uncle Niviaqsi was still single in those days and was happy to take care of the young girl. He would take bits of driftwood from the shore and carve her figurines and boats as toys, or he would make her toy *qamutiks* (sleds). All these things provided her with many happy hours to which Kenojuak still thinks back with joy, and a touch of nostalgia, too.

Experiencing the harsh conditions of life in the Arctic gives the Inuit a different, a more direct relationship to death than we *qallunaat* (non-Inuit people) generally possess. Their acceptance of death stems, by no means, from indifference or equanimity, but from their experience of death as a fate encountered in their daily lives, and with which they learn how to deal. Kenojuak, too, was repeatedly confronted with death and dying, but although the loss of loved ones was distressing and in many cases deeply incisive, she became increasingly familiar with death each time it struck.

When her aunt Tayaraq passed away unexpectedly, Kenojuak, then eight years old, observed very sharply what was done with the dead woman, and was deeply impressed. The women of the camp carefully washed the dead body and braided her long, dark hair to a plait that began over her forehead. Then they wrapped the body in a large woollen blanket and laid it down in the tundra far away, with its face to the sky. After that, they carefully piled layer upon layer of stones over the body to form a stone mound. It is a lonely burial place, rarely visited by humans any more.

As a child, Kenojuak often walked over old burial grounds where the bones of people long deceased lay strewn over rocks and tundra – a sign of predatory animals. The children were afraid of the spirits of their ancestors and often started whistling to 'blow away' the supernatural being from their hands.

Years later, when walking in the Kangiaq area, where the relics of an old camp of her ancestors could still be found, Kenojuak chanced across the grave of an unknown hunter from the distant past. Inuit snow goggles and an ancient stone knife were laid carefully beside the skull. This encounter with the loneliness of death and the transience of life was another that made a lasting impression on her.

In those days, the men used their light *kayaks* to travel and hunt on the water. On short trips they occasionally took women and children along as well; while the children disappeared in inside the *kayak*, the women would sit at the bow, stretching their legs out to keep the *kayak* balanced. Normally, however, women and children were transported in the larger *umiaq*, the 'women's boat.' In connection with marine hunting, Kenojuak recalls another special occurrence. One day, her stepfather Tapaungai was constructing the wooden frame for his *kayak*, when a whale was sighted. The other men pursued it in their *kayaks* and drove it closer and closer to land. Tapaungai grabbed his rifle, too, and when the whale had come close enough, he fired from the shore and wounded it mortally. Aiming to harpoon the whale before it sank to the depths, Tapaungai jumped onto the *kayak* frame that still had no hide stretched over it and paddled bravely out to sea. He stuck his harpoon deep into the whale and attached the usual sealskin balloon as a float so that the whale would not be lost.

Nowadays, whale meat has become a rare delight for the Inuit, who still consider *maktaaq* – the skin of the whale and the blubber directly underneath it – to be a special delicacy. It contains a higher concentration of ascorbic acid, vitamin C, than citrus fruits. Being invited to a traditional 'Maktaaq Feast' is a very special honour.

In those days, the Inuit were already obtaining much of their food from the trading posts of the Hudson's Bay Company; the only sweets for children, however, were candies and chewing gum, as we learn from Kenojuak. The Company used to grant loans to the hunters and trappers on generous terms, and handed out 'food stamps,' a kind of coupon; accounts where settled on delivery of fox furs whereby distinctions were made according to the species of fox and the particular sub-species. When Kenojuak was still a young girl, all types of fox fur found a buyer, but blue fox furs, a rarity, achieved the highest counter-value.[10]

Generally speaking, individual families did not stay in the same camp and group on a permanent basis. Depending on external living conditions, it was quite common to change location repeatedly and to move to other relatives in a different camp, often far away. Kenojuak and her relatives did not reside continuously in Camp Sapujjuaq either. Depending on the game available, they moved to other camps under the leadership of Tagatuk, her grandmother's brother, or with her uncle Tikituk. Tikituk had married his step-cousin Lucy shortly before: when her father died, Lucy had been only four years old, and her mother subsequently married Tagatuk. At that time, Tagatuk had a wooden boat moved by paddles and a canvas sail. On calm days with no wind, the boat moved through the water very slowly, even when everybody used their paddle. Tagatuk himself had carved the paddles from driftwood he had found on the shore.

Tayaraq died in the spring of 1935. When fall came, her surviving husband, Tapaungai, got married again – to Kenojuak's mother, Silaqqi. Four children were born of the marriage.

Not long after their wedding, Tapaungai and Silaqqi left Sapujjuaq and moved to Camp Igalaalik ('where a window opens in the ice'), where Tapaungai's brother Ashoona lived with Pitseolak. Kenojuak, however, then eight, who had grown very close to her grandmother, stayed with her in Camp Sapujjuaq and they continued living in the same tent. She tells us that her bonds to Quitsaq were much stronger than to her mother, Silaqqi. Her brother Adamie was meanwhile living with his uncle Niviaqsi, who had married Kunu shortly before.

Now and then, Kenojuak would set out with some friends to Camp Igalaalik to visit her relatives and stay with them for a few weeks. At the age of ten or eleven, she was staying there once again. One spring day she went for a sled ride across the sea ice. Others in the group were her older sister Qimiqpikuluk, her brother Adamie and Iqaluk [Echalook], an experienced hunter who was keeping an eye on the children. They wanted to look for the eggs of nesting seagulls. As they travelled across the ice, wide cracks kept opening up in the ice before them, criss-crossing through the ice over considerable distances and allowing them to look down into the blackish blue water below. Everything seemed calm and peaceful.

Suddenly, in one of the cracks in the ice, Kenojuak saw a head with very, very long black flowing hair; she discerned a strange being that sank slowly into the deep before her eyes. When she cried out, Adamie lifted his rifle, but Iqaluk fiercely stopped him. Everyone realized then that Talilayuk, that legendary goddess of all sea creatures, had revealed herself to them. Filled with fear and terror at this unexpected manifestation, the four of them returned hastily to camp.

In reply to our questions, Kenojuak tells us that, since then, she has looked into the deep black fissures in cracking ice many times without trepidation. But Talilayuk never appeared to her again.

Kenojuak has many stories to tell about that period in her life - for instance: she was to learn together with one of her young uncles how to drive and control a dog team. The first lesson was to jump skilfully from a moving *qamutik* (sled), run along beside it and then jump back on again. The *qamutik* was drawn by a dog team in a fan-like arrangement, with gang leads of different lengths; it was important to have a good lead dog because the animals running in the team were engaged in a perpetual contest with each other.

Once Kenojuak was given the task of supervising the dogs and keeping them quiet while her uncle was stalking a bearded seal. The dogs always got very excited when their 'master' aimed his rifle, but only after the shot rang out were they allowed to start running. However, when her uncle got ready to fire, Kenojuak was unable to keep the dogs under control. They jumped around wildly and the seal escaped. The girl felt rather embarrassed because the seal hunt came to nothing, and to top it all she had got completely soaked by melt-water when trying to catch the dogs.

She was always very sad when she had to stay behind in the camp and the seal hunt took place without her; if she was allowed to go along, however, she would get terribly excited. In her own words, "It was wonderful living in this way. But watching over the dogs and having to keep them quiet when someone was stalking a seal – I didn't like that at all."

Here is another story featuring dogs. One spring day, the whole family was travelling from Camp Igalaalik to visit the grandmother in Sapujjuaq. The uncles went by canoe while Kenojuak and her older sister Qimmikpikaluk took the dog sled. Kenojuak remembers well the happiness she felt. Once, when her sister was obviously having trouble getting the dogs to turn in a certain direction, Kenojuak sensed the challenge of driving the team the way she wanted – and succeeded.

But when they had reached the camp, and the girls were applauded by all for their achievement, the two of them ran into grandmother's tent and hid away; after all, at the time they were first put in charge of a dog team, they were still very young and shy.

When they left the camp again, two men were assigned to drive the sled because the big sister was not quite able to control the dogs. Kenojuak was terribly disappointed – even though she had managed to steer the dogs in the right direction, the adults apparently had no confidence in her succeeding a second time.

The third dog story goes like this. One spring day, she and her aunt Kanaaqbalik, her mother's younger sister, were travelling with the dog team to Camp Sapujjuaq, where one of their caches was located. The men had already launched the canoes. The two were proud of doing this trip without help from the menfolk, especially since Kenojuak's companion was carrying a baby in her *amautiq*. They even decided to check the fox traps on the way.

They were already on the way back to Igalaalik when Kenojuak suddenly remembered a harpoon tip they had left behind in Sapujjuaq. Her aunt was unable to restrain the dogs, so once again it was up to Kenojuak to manoeuvre the team round and head back the way they had come. Hardly had she untangled the leads and brought the dogs under control, when suddenly, without warning, the whole pack dashed off to the seashore, where a seal was basking in the sun. The lead dog sank its teeth into the seal and tried to hang onto it, but the seal escaped. The whole spectacle ended with much laughter – although the two were sad at losing the seal.

Kallusiqbik:
Johnniebo's courting and Kenojuak's initial reluctance

In 1945 – Silaqqi had moved away a long time before – Quitsaq, too, left Camp Sapujjuaq and travelled with her daughter Kanaaqbalik and her daughter's husband to Natsilik Lake (Nettilling Lake). In those days, there were caribou in abundance at this largest lake situated farther north on Baffin Island; more importantly, there were relatives of Quitsaq staying in one of the lakeshore camps whom she wanted to see again after so many years. With several heavily loaded dog sleds, the travellers succeeded in putting the long and arduous journey behind them.

With Quitsaq gone, Kenojuak went to live with her mother in Camp Igalaalik. Little joy was in store, however, because Tapaungai, Silaqqi's second husband, died soon after in the spring of 1946, following a severe illness that bore heavily upon all those near to him. So Kenojuak was happy when her grandmother returned after a year to her son Tikituk and his wife, Lucy, in Camp Sapujjuaq. From then on, she lived with her beloved grandmother again. Quitsaq had left Nettilling Lake when many people died during a flu epidemic, among them her son-in-law and Ashoona, the husband of Pitseolak Ashoona.

For various reasons, Kenojuak has many deeply ingrained memories of that summer in 1946. Felix Conrad died then, the manager of the Cape Dorset trading post operated by the Baffin Trading Company (BTC). He had distilled his own spirits made from tundra berries, raisins and other dried fruits, keeping the concoction in methanol cans. Unfortunately, he got the different cans mixed up once, reached for the wrong one and, as a result, died of methanol poisoning.

When he was found, he was lying across the threshold of the warehouse – an important omen for the Inuit. For this reason, he was not buried in the local cemetery but beside a path leading up a hill that overlooked the settlement. Since then, it has been legend among the settlement inhabitants that his spirit continues to wander Cape Dorset. Even fifty years later, people still talk of one Felix Conrad, claiming he invested much energy in expanding the BTC building and coated the walls with moss to insulate them against the cold – an ideal nesting place for lemmings. When the building was finally demolished, someone discovered a bottle of gin he had inadvertently left behind.

Conrad had once requested Peter Pitseolak for the hand of his daughter, Udluriak, in marriage, but was turned down. Pitseolak later consented that his daughter marry Tommy Manning, a manager at Hudson's Bay Company. One of the children born of that marriage was our Inuktitut interpreter, Jeannie Manning, who assisted us in many conversations with Kenojuak; Jimmy Manning, manager at West Baffin Eskimo Co-operative, is her adopted brother. Udluriak died of a heart attack in 1971, at the age of only forty-seven, a rare cause of death among the Inuit then as now.

The Baffin Trading Company commenced operations in Cape Dorset in 1939 under the management of one James Cantley, a former employee of Hudson's Bay Company; the Baring Brothers Bank (Newfoundland) had put up the required capital. This provided the Inuit with an alternative means of bartering their furs. Moreover, the BTC traded not only in fox furs, but also in seal skin and polar bear furs, even in walrus skin. In contrast, the Hudson's Bay Company had previously only accepted select fox furs. Before the new competitor came, the Hudson's Bay Company had used its monopoly to dictate the prices and the specific types of fur in which it was prepared to trade (for example, prior to 1939 it paid a mere five Canadian dollars for a fur, the counter-value being less than ten fish hooks). The market now became more open, and a good livelihood could be earned during a normal hunting season.

In 1948-49, however, when the Baffin Trading Company was compelled for economic reasons to close down its three eastern Arctic trading posts in Inukjuak, Salluit (Sugluk) and Cape Dorset, the Inuit were once again dependent on a single trading partner. This experience taught them the benefits to be obtained by setting up a co-operative of their own, but more of that later.

The second crucial event to occur in 1946, and by far the more important for Kenojuak, was that, only recently returned to her grandmother, she lost forever the sense of warmth and protectedness in her camp. At that time, an Inuit childhood was still very short. Young girls, especially, tended to wed at an early age, and traditionally had no say in the choice of husband. Marriage often served to strengthen the bond between two families. Friends have confirmed to us from their own experience that, even in the 1970s, arranged marriages for newborn babies were by no means unusual. On the other hand, less and less importance is attached nowadays to keeping such promises – young people are ignoring such traditions to an increasing extent and pursue their own goals in life.

Kenojuak had now been living in Camp Sapujjuaq for fifteen years; by then she was nineteen years old and long since of marrying age. Although she had not been betrothed to anyone as a young child, she was not consulted when it came to the choice of husband. Instead, she noticed from all manner of signs that she could anticipate some kind of arrangement being made as to a suitable spouse for her, and was scared at the prospect of having to marry soon.

One summer day, she was asleep in her grandmother's *qarmaq* when a number of visitors arrived in the camp, among them a man by the name of Towkie, and his wife, Elisapee. They came as envoys of Towkie's brother Johnniebo, who wanted to take Kenojuak for his wife. Kenojuak pretended to sleep while the new arrivals discussed the matter with her mother and her uncles. The negotiations were brief, the participants quickly agreeing that the match was a promising one. Johnniebo himself was not present; in those days, a suitor was never allowed to be present at the first round of negotiations.

Kenojuak could well remember Johnniebo – she had seen him in Cape Dorset, and she could also remember how he had teased her in a friendly way. However imposing he may have been as a personality, even as a young man, to Kenojuak he looked like a *qallunaaq* (a white man). In her own words, "I found him repulsive, and I was not looking forward in the slightest to being married to him." She may have had no other choice, once the marriage was settled, but her attitude was moved by the stubborn thought, "*You* picked him out, so *you* may marry him!"

We talk with her about the change in customs that has been occurring among the Inuit as well. Before the missionaries came, it was the families that determined which children would become man and wife. Occasionally, an unbetrothed young man would also ask his relatives to ask parents for the hand of their daughter. Weddings were an unceremonious affair. The only change brought about by Christianization was that couples were now wedded in a Christian ceremony whenever a priest came to the area. When public administration was finally established in the region, marriages were officially registered – firstly by RCMP officers, later by the local authorities. Nowadays, there are many couples who live together without getting married; that way, they feel less tied down and less burdened with responsibilities. Kenojuak takes a divided stance on this issue. On the one hand, she would like traditions to be preserved, yet she also shows understanding for the way young people behave. Having said this, however, she states that she completely rejects the avoidance of all responsibility on the part of some. When she was young, girls resisted being married off, and, laughing, she continues, "If things were like in the old days and the men had to officially request the hand of a girl in marriage, the menfolk would be in a sorry state. Because the girls would not be as easily gotten as they are today. In any case, the ties binding two people to each other were much more stable in those days!"

Later on in that summer of 1946, people from the surrounding camps came together in Cape Dorset, among them Kenojuak and Johnniebo. After the break-up of the ice and navigation channels opened up, everybody was awaiting with growing excitement and full of expectation the arrival of the *Nascopie* supply ship. This annual event was also a longed-for occasion to see relatives and friends again. And as everywhere in the Arctic the ship's arrival in summer was celebrated with a big feast, the *umiaqjuakkanak* (the time of the big ship).

Anyone who was capable would help unload the cargo; the goods were brought to the beach in small boats and carried to the warehouse. Work was followed by the *palajut* (throwing and catching), i.e. the manager of the Hudson's Bay Company would throw packages of tea, biscuits, sweets and other kinds of food, as well as tobacco products and thick socks, from the warehouse roof to the throngs of the Inuit waiting below as payment for their help.

Due to the spread of tuberculosis, the government at that time had ordered all Inuit people to be X-rayed aboard the ship; Kenojuak, too, was made to stand before the X-ray machine for the first time.

When the *Nascopie* left harbour to deliver supplies to the other settlements, Kenojuak also left Cape Dorset together with Johnniebo. As was custom among the Inuit, she had been made his wife without any form of ceremony.

In the first weeks of their conjugal community, Kenojuak must have proved a very unruly young wife for Johnniebo indeed. In speaking to us, she particularly emphasizes the fact that she was "very sharp-tongued." Whenever Johnniebo came closer, she would throw pebbles at him. But he refused to take this behaviour too seriously, laughed in his good-natured way and kept up his own courteous efforts to take care of her. Kenojuak felt how much he loved her and that he was faithfully devoted to her. She liked this warm-hearted and kind man more and more as the days progressed, and he became the love of her life. "He was a faithful man, of which there is only one in many thousands!"

Johnniebo was born in 1923 and named after his grandmother's husband. It seems that his ancestors had originally settled around Cumberland Sound, primarily in the Pangnirtung area. There is documentary evidence that they had come into closer contact with North American whalers as far back as the mid-19th century, and that they had travelled far on their ships; for example, his great-grandfather, Kadlarjuk, died on a return voyage from the United States. Johnniebo's grandmother, Annie Qimmaluq, born around 1850 as the daughter of Kadlarjuk, had also often travelled on whaling ships in Cumberland Sound, in Frobisher Bay and the Hudson Strait; like many other Inuit, she used to help out in gutting and cleaning the catch, which in those days were still big. A girl was born of her liaison with one of the whaler captains, a *qallunaaq* called Walker; she named the child Kadlarjuk in memory of her own father.

Soon after, around 1875, Annie Qimmaluq married an Inuk by the name of Qimuakjuk. According to the handed-down portrayal of the man, he must have been an important and much-respected leader. He is also said to have been a shaman, something that he himself always denied. Owing to his skilfulness and hunting prowess, he possessed whaling boats of his own – sufficient reason for some Inuit to envy him intensely. He was greatly respected among white whalers, however, who called him John, Johnny or 'Mate.' A *qallunaaq* is supposed to have asked once, "Where is Johnny's boat?", from which the Inuit then derived 'Johnniebo.'

Around the turn of the year in 1888-89, Johnniebo was murdered by Inuit. To this day, the elders in Cape Dorset (for example, Osuitok Ipeelee and Pauta Saila) recount what they heard from their parents. The primary motive for the murder seems indeed to have been jealousy and envy of his successes and his connections to *qallunaat*. A cardinal role was obviously played by the leader of a small clique by the name of Alainga; it was he who later married Johnniebo's widow, a step that was quite common among the Inuit at the time.[11]

In the end, Annie Qimmaluq settled with her family and relatives in the Kimmirut area. She worked for a while for the Hudson's Bay Company in Cape Dorset, where she treated furs and skins the Company had bought up. Now and again, people would use her services as an interpreter because it was thought, since she had sailed to the land of the white men, that she could speak and understand the language of the *qallunaat*. Yet she understood little more than the other Inuit.

Her daughter Kadlarjuk married Ashevak, and together they had six children, one of whom was Kenojuak's husband, Johnniebo. Kadlarjuk excelled as a versatile musician; she was equally proficient on the accordion and the fiddle. These musical talents were inherited by her daughter Aggeok, who became the second wife of Peter Pitseolak in 1941. The musical instruments had been brought to the country by Scottish whalers around the turn of the century and later donated to the Inuit. From these whalers the Inuit also learned how to make bannock,[12] a kind of fried bread that rose in popularity to become a staple food.

In that summer of 1946, Johnniebo and Kenojuak travelled in a boat belonging to a hunter friend of theirs to Camp Kallusiqbik on Saqbak Bay, where Johnniebo's brother, Towkie, and a number of other families lived. Like everywhere else, the women were generally responsible for ensuring that everyday life in the camp ran smoothly. Their work included preparing and processing meat, tending to and bringing up the children, making and repairing clothes and preparing skins, including scraping and stretching them. The semicircular *ulu* (woman's knife) and the scraper were items that a woman could not get by without.

The men were mainly preoccupied with hunting, in order to provide sufficient food for their people and dogs. The snowstorms that occurred almost daily for months on end meant that even a skilled hunter could only succeed if the ice permitted. Of course, the men had to keep their equipment in good condition; indispensable items such as harpoons and *qamutiks* (sleds) often had to be made or repaired. They were also responsible for building the dwellings, be they igloos or *qarmaqs*. Most decisions concerning the organization and relocating of camps were a male preserve, too.

While the men mostly went fishing and hunting in the days following their arrival, the women in the camp made preparations for the impending winter months. Children and youths climbed the surrounding hills and gathered blueberries in the tundra. Before the first frost, Kenojuak gathered moss just like she had done in her grandmother's camp. She needed the moss as a wick for her *qulliq*. Quitsaq had also shown Kenojuak how to enhance the flame by mixing the chopped moss with fuzz from willow blossoms. She used the sliced off top of a tobacco tin, perforated with nails, as a grater for cutting the moss into tiny pieces. This powdery moss was spread in a narrow strip along the straight edge of the *qulliq* and soaked in oil from seal blubber. The wick thus produced was easy to light, and not only did its flame spread a cosy warmth, but also served for 'cooking' and for drying wet clothes. Tending the *qulliq* was a typical household chore for Inuit women. Even while others slept at night, they would tend the flames with charred sticks of wood. Furthermore, it was quite common for the menfolk to take small *qulliqs* and a supply of moss with them when laying traps and hunting in order to warm their hands and to dry their clothing in their igloo at the end of the day.

Kiattuuq and Saatturittuq:
Young mother

Kenojuak's time with Johnniebo in their first shared camp at Saqbak Bay was to prove all too short, in that fall of 1946. Snow had already spread a white blanket over the earth, but the sea had not yet frozen over when Peter Pitseolak sent his Peterhead boat to Saqbak Bay.

In January 1946, he had suddenly been taken to hospital in Winnipeg for treatment of an infectious kidney disease and was now returning in fall. He gave up the full-time job he had held over previous years at the Baffin Trading Company in Cape Dorset, and directed his relatives to come and stay with him in his Camp Kiattuuq. At that, Johnniebo and Kenojuak left the shores of Saqbak Bay with Johnniebo's brother Towkie and his family.

Kiattuuq is not far from Cape Dorset, still within eyesight of Kinngait's rounded crest, so it was not far from here to the next trading centre. For the Inuit, however, there was another aspect of greater importance, namely the direct access to the open sea and its marine hunting grounds. Kenojuak describes Kiattuuq as a wonderful, beautiful area with sloping hillsides teeming with vegetation, undulating hills and countless lakes. Their ancestors had lived on the shores of these lakes, as evidenced by the remains of 'Tunik' homes long since abandoned – overgrown tent rings, whale bones strewn about, hollows in the ground, and graves. The Inuit call the people of the Dorset culture 'Tuniks,' who lived on Baffin Island until around A.D. 1300, and who were then either absorbed or pushed out by the Thule Eskimos – the direct ancestors of today's Inuit – that migrated here from the Bering Strait. We often heard of how unusually strong but simple-minded the Tuniks were. Peter Pitseolak tells of an unusually large Tunik grave near his Camp Kiattuq, at the sight of which he always asked himself who might be buried in it.

At the end of 1946, there were ten families living in Camp Kiattuuq under the leadership of Peter Pitseolak: Pitseolak himself with his wife and children, his brother Qavavau and his family, Kadlarjuk, the mother of his wife Aggeok, as well as Aggeok's brothers, namely Towkie with his wife Elisapee, and Johnniebo with Kenojuak. On the other side of the hill, in dwellings that hugged a narrow cliff, lived the other families, including some Inuit who later became well-known artists – Kopapik and his wife Mary, as well as Natsivak and Kalai.

As we talk Kenojuak adds that Natsivak died in 1962 on the journey to the medical centre in Cape Dorset, where she was hoping, in vain, to receive medical help at the very last moment. The life of Kopapik and that of two of his relatives was plotted out in 1969 after they had eaten improperly preserved seal meat.

During the first winter in Kiattuuq, Johnniebo and Kenojuak were compelled to live the whole time in an igloo; they were already too far into the cold season to build a *qarmaq*, as each of them was actually accustomed. Johnniebo built their igloo, five metres in diameter, when the snow had reached the right consistency. To stop the meltwater dripping down, they fastened a tent canvas inside the igloo to wooden stakes that they had driven through the blocks of snow. The window was a block of clear freshwater ice. A chimney made of snow, on which they spread water to freeze, led through a hole in the tent canvas and the wall of snow.

It was important to Peter Pitseolak that he be looked upon as a leader who set high standards, and he expected a high level of performance and loyal cooperation from the men in the camp. All the trapping equipment belonged to him. Even though many foxes were caught by mutual effort, he would not dream of sharing the furs with the men of camp or let them have a little of the catch.

At that time, Johnniebo was one of the youngest men in the camp and had to accept a place of subordinate rank. He saw no prospects in the foreseeable future of strengthening his position in the camp. On top of that, his possessions were rather meagre, he had only a few traps he could call his own, and was therefore barely able to earn a sufficient livelihood from fox trapping to support himself and his wife, not to speak of improving their economic status. However, the camp provided all its inhabitants with a modicum of security, so he felt obliged to stay, albeit reluctantly.

The date of July 21, 1947 is one that all Inuit living in Sikusiilaq at that time remember to this day. About two kilometres to the east of Cape Dorset island, in the vicinity of Beacon Island, the *Nascopie* struck a reef on the sea bed that was not marked on the sea charts, and tore a large hole in the hull. The ship stayed on the reef for months until it eventually disappeared from view. Almost half a century passed before divers examined the wreck lying on the sea bed. For Peter Pitseolak and the other inhabitants of his camp, also Johnniebo and Kenojuak, the sinking of the *Nascopie* was an event of great significance, and thanks to his descriptions we know of some remarkable details that Kenojuak confirms to us.[13]

Every year in summer, when the *Nascopie* arrived with supplies, there was always plenty to eat. The ship's cook obviously had a soft touch for the Inuit waiting at the landing stage and made sure they were given everything imaginable. The actual name of the cook was irrelevant, people just called him 'Storekeeper!'. He pulled out everything he could get his hands on – corned beef, stew, simply everything. Everybody ate outdoors, of course, because there was no other suitable place. When the ship showed up on the horizon, people would flock down from all sides to Cape Dorset and help unload the cargo two or three days long. The supply ship was the principal means of transport at that time. Air transport was still considered too expensive by most, and so the *Nascopie* usually brought all the merchandise for the Hudson's Bay trading post. Anyone unable to help with the unloading would prepare at the beach the food for those doing the carrying and received pay for this like all the others.

In 1946, the previous ship's cook was replaced by another. All of a sudden, no food was given to the Inuit, who felt rather unwanted in general. Peter Pitseolak, who was obviously respected, was the only one invited to dine by the new cook. Additionally, one year later, command of the ship was transferred to a new captain.

When the *Nascopie* approached Cape Dorset on that July 21, 1947, the Hudson's Bay manager advised the new captain by radio that he should take Pitseolak, a man who knew the waters well, on board as pilot to guide them. The captain tersely rejected the advice, apparently convinced that he knew everything himself. Peter Pitseolak comments, "If I had steered the ship, it would never have gone aground. I had been steering the ship for three or four years. The new captain did not want me to meet the ship."

Since the day was particularly beautiful, Peter Pitseolak went out seal hunting. He was after fresh meat, and since the captain had decided to forego on his assistance, he saw no reason why he should not enjoy some good hunting. Two seals were his reward. On the way back to Cape Dorset, he and his companions saw that the ship was rather high in the water. As it turned out, it had hit the rock and was now sitting high at low tide. When the seal hunters reached the shore, they were greeted with the words, "Our supply ship has run aground." Pitseolak cajoled in return, "Then we will take all her possessions!" At that time, he had no inkling as yet that the ship had struck a leak and that his joking reply was nearer the mark than he had thought.

When the tide rose again that night and the ship had torn itself away from the rock, someone was sent to ask Pitseolak to come and help immediately; suddenly he was needed after all. On the way out by boat to the damaged ship, the helpers came across a large barque full of *qallunaat* – people who had travelled here on the *Nascopie* and were now rowing to shore. They shouted across that the ship had a large hole in its hull. Pitseolak was the only one to understand what had happened; his companions could hear nothing but the noise of the engine. When Pitseolak shouted to his companions what he had heard, the Hudson's Bay manager wanted to simply call off the rescue, but Pitseolak admonished him, saying, "You cannot do that! We must go; there are still people there – they are flashing lights because they want our help."

Once at the supply ship, the Bay manager had to make it clear to the captain that "Peter has come to the *Nascopie* to help." Only then did he finally let him come on board. The crew was trying in vain to bail the water out of the hull. At the same time, they also threw coal for the ship's engines over board. To make matters even worse, it had started to rain in the meantime, and so the captain asked the helpers to come into his cabin. He had already put out 'strong water,' whisky. Pitseolak did not want to get drunk, and so he poured the contents of his glass into a bucket when the captain once turned his back. The Bay manager also poured his drink away, so as not to befuddle himself.

After moving to and from, the captain admitted defeat. "Okay, Pitseolak, then you steer the ship!" The anchor was lifted, and the ship got under way. Pitseolak first steered the ship in the opposite direction to it's proper course in order to get away from the shallows, but the captain soon stopped him, "Don't let us run too far into deep water!" As Pitseolak later realized, the ship had already begun to sink slowly. The *qallunaat* were aware of the fact, but they wanted to keep it a secret from the Inuk; he should try his best first of all.

Pitseolak then steered the ship around 180 degrees, thus putting them back on the correct route. The shallows were behind them, and Pitseolak said to the captain that they should now go full speed ahead. He had hardly uttered the words when they started moving astern. Pitseolak asked a few times, disbelievingly, "What's going on? You're travelling in the wrong direction!" He did not understand why the *qallunaat* were not doing everything they could to rescue the ship and its cargo. In the end, the Bay manager answered with resignation in his voice, "Its all pointless!"

They moved the stern onto a small island and finally managed to run the ship aground again. The captain had given up all hope long before and was convinced that, were they to steam onwards, the ship would surely sink before reaching the pier at Cape Dorset.

More and more water was gushing in and the ship was listing. The lifeboats were all launched with utmost speed. Pitseolak – the only Inuk on board – was also told to get into one of the boats. When he was leaving the ship, the engines of the *Nascopie* were already flooded by water. For a while it seemed as though the captain wanted to stay on board. And only after the Bay manager vehemently threatened for leaving the ship, did he finally climbd into one of the lifeboats, the last one to cast off. All the *Nascopie* boats made it to the safety of shore, where the first *qallunaat* to have left the ship were waiting for them.

A few hours later, the *Avatuk* (her real name was the *M/V MacLean*) appeared on the scene and helped the shipwrecked sailors. The Inuit from far about who had sped to the island in their boats – including Peter Pitseolak's brother Pootoogook – helped get the men embarked. Having got that far, the *qallunaat* held Peter Pitseolak back and waited until Pootoogook and the remaining Inuit had returned to the shore. Turning to Pitseolak, they commanded him, "Get cracking and take as much off the wreck as your boat can carry!"

Pitseolak describes what happened next:[14]

> Soon my boat was full; it was not a small boat.... It was a happy time – until we reached shore. When we reached shore it turned out that we were to be scolded. My brother Pootoogook was upset because he, too, wanted things from the ship. It was unpleasant. He scolded us for taking things which he wanted himself. But I was the one who was to take what I wanted.
>
> Our boss [the Hudson's Bay manager] came to meet us on the shore. When he saw things he especially liked, he told lies. He said, "That's my order." I was being pretty soft and giving things away. That's why there were many people at the shore meeting us. Then, all of a sudden, I got angry. I told the boss, "These are all yours! Take them all – all the things in the boat!" I told him all this and then he left us alone.
>
> There was also a silly policeman from Lake Harbour. He was also taking what he liked – taking things away from us. It was greedy. I told him he was taking the possessions of the Eskimos and then he slowed down his grabbing....

But even the people from the other side, from Eenookjuak [Inukjuak] – Port Harrison – came. They, too, came to collect from the ship. There were three boats. … Also people came from Lake Harbour [Kimmirut]. … Maybe the people from Port Harrison did not collect too much but the people from Cape Dorset gave them some of their collections. They couldn't collect themselves from the ship because when they came the *Nascopie* was half sunk.

People in the South heard about us. Our Bay boss wrote a letter which told lies about us. In his letter he said, "They are not hunting for fox any more – they are just sitting down because now they are rich." I did not like this at all. He told lies. We were hunting for fox; what he wrote was not true. He was wrong. Some people do not even try to be truthful.

With the help of his men, Johnniebo among them, Peter Pitseolak managed to stuff his Peterhead boat with wood, coal and many other things from the wreck before taking everything back to Camp Kiattuq, where he lived. That fall, with the material salvaged from the *Nascopie*, he built himself a sturdy timber house. The front door bore the words 'Chief Steward' and behind the porthole windows there stood three bath tubs, the perfect place to cut open and slice up seal meat.

As long as his supply lasted, namely two winters, he heated the house by burning coal. After that, however, Pitseolak lived in his comfortable house during the summers only, preferring to spend the cold season in a traditional *qarmaq*, where temperatures could be kept more pleasant than in the large house. People ridiculed his bad investment for a long time after. "But maybe they just envied him," Kenojuak adds with a laugh.

In the year the *Nascopie* was lost, that is, a year after she had been wed to Johnniebo, Kenojuak became pregnant with their first child. The women in the camp gave her plenty of good advice and let her know about many precautions she should take. For example, she learned that chewing gum would cause the baby to be born with a sticky layer on its skin. When twisting wool, she should make sure she didn't make a noose otherwise the unborn child could strangle itself on its umbilical cord.

Her mother-in-law spoke to her about various pre-natal taboos that had still been of practical importance a generation before. In those days, a woman in labour with her first child stayed alone in a *qarmaq* or igloo built solely for this purpose. Years before, her mother-in-law had herself sat on a caribou skin in a small, roofless igloo, with nothing else but water to quench her thirst, and gave birth to her child with no outside help. She tied the umbilical cord with caribou sinews and buried the afterbirth. Returning to her kin was not permitted until the baby's umbilical cord had fallen off, which meant she was left to her own devices for several days on end.

Fortunately for Kenojuak, there was no need to obey such customs any longer. It was fall. Snow covered the tundra, but ice had not yet formed. Four women who were to act as her midwives during her period in labour were ordered to Kenojuak's *qarmaq*. Nobody else was allowed to enter the *qarmaq* once the contractions started. While she knelt on the caribou skin, two of them pinned down her arms to be on the safe side, while another pressed her knee into Kenojuak's back.

Kenojuak's first child was a boy. Johnniebo called him Jamasie after his brother, who had died as a young man. Kenojuak carried the child around in her *amautiq* everywhere she went; an intimate and affectionate bond arose between them. For the young mother, this was a very happy time.

Even in the mid-20th century, a woman and her children had to bear considerable hardship if there was no male adult to fully support them; this was the reason Kenojuak's mother, Silaqqi, entered a new partnership the same year, 1947, with Nuvualia, the brother of Johnniebo's father, Ashevak.

When we speak with Kenojuak in somewhat more detail about this relationship between Johnniebo's uncle, Nuvualia, and her mother, we learn that Parr, a highly respected artist in the settlement even today who became famous during the last years of his life, was another of Ashevak's brothers, and, therefore, an uncle of Johnniebo's. Almost as an aside, we hear about an event in Parr's past, an example of the 'wife-swapping' that was by no means rare among the Inuit 'in the old days.' It was like this: Parr's parents had arranged for him to be married to a girl named Ningeukaluk, but Parr did not take much of a fancy to his young wife. When Pootoogook proposed that they exchange wives, he consented without further ado, especially since no children had been born of the marriage. Pootoogook gave his half-sister Eleeshushe to Parr as his new wife, receiving Ningeukaluk in return. We have not heard since of any other cases of wife-swapping.

Silaqqi and Nuvualia moved to the Kimmirut (Lake Harbour) area and settled there. In 1949, Silaqqi gave birth to another child, a daughter, Iqalik, who lives today in Cape Dorset, separated from her husband, Elijah Pootoogook.

In that winter of 1947, Johnniebo and the other men were much involved in setting traps. At other times they hunted for seals again at the flow edge.

Seals were hunted either at *aglus* (breathing holes in the ice), from the flow edge or from boats on the water. The seal keeps its breathing holes open by coming up to the ice surface again and again. An Inuit hunter uses a probe to find these holes that might have been covered over with snow.

He will often stoop for hours over the hole, motionless, until he hears the sound of breath escaping or the movement of the piece of down serving as an indicator. Fast as lightning, he rams the harpoon into the *aglu* in the hope of hitting the seal. If successful, he will pull the seal out onto the ice through the *aglu*. This is not so easy in the case of a bearded seal, *ujjuk*, and he will need help from several men to heave the animal out of the water since it can weigh up to three or four hundred kilograms.

In the spring, when the seals are attracted to the warmth of the sun shining on the ice, they are much easier prey for Inuit hunters. The latter then try, often camouflaged by a shield of white canvas, to stalk up on a seal lying on the ice in order to shoot or harpoon it before it slips back into the water.

In the summer of 1948, all the Inuit in the area set out to Cape Dorset to await the arrival of a special ship that was coming to carry out medical and dental examinations of the population. X-ray screening was conducted once again, as well as other medical tests. Many had to remain on the ship because of signs of disease, and were taken farther south to hospitals and sanatoria where they were treated for serious diseases, including tuberculosis in particular.

In those days Quitsaq, Kenojuak's grandmother, blind in one eye and tormented by arthritis, was living with her youngest daughter, Kanaaqbalik. When travelling from her camp to Cape Dorset she fell dangerously ill and died on the way; she was buried in the settlement.

Nineteen forty-eight also marked the end of the Baffin Trading Company (BTC) in Cape Dorset. The same year, family allowances were introduced. The money was initially paid out by the Hudson's Bay Company and relieved many cases of acute distress.

In those days, collecting annual statistics about births, marriages and deaths on behalf of the government was still the responsibility of officers on the supply ships but this work was later performed by officials in the Royal Canadian Mounted Police (RCMP) and other local government officials. Until then, Inuit people generally had only one name, the one they received at birth. In bygone days, newborns were not given their names by their parents, but by the camp or settlement elders. The birth name provided no clues as to whether the child in question was a boy or a girl – names were frequently chosen in memory of someone recently deceased. Now, with the introduction of statistics, every Inuk was assigned an official identity number. Kenojuak's was E 7 - 1035, and for many years this was her only official designation. 'E' stood for *E*ast of Gjoa Haven; the number 7 represented the Cape Dorset region, while the four-digit number referred to the person herself. This degrading system was not abandoned until 1968 to 1970, when the Inuit could choose their own surnames.

In March 1949, an Anglican missionary from Kimmirut (Lake Harbour) visited the scattered camps in the area by dog sled. He also came to Kiattuuq, where he celebrated the Church wedding of Johnniebo and Kenojuak in Peter Pitseolak's timber house. The following evening, their boy was christened.

Peter Pitseolak was in his element. He was one of the first Inuit to possess a camera and he photographed just about everything he could. Kenojuak received a picture of the young priest sitting at the table in Peter's house.

Johnniebo and Kenojuak spent the following summer in Camp Saatturittuq on Sartowitok Bay. The area was well-known for the particularly large numbers of ptarmigan to be found there. But that was not their real reason for changing to a camp where various relatives had previously moved to – Johnniebo was tired of having to submit to Pitseolak's will and, what is more, being dependent on his benevolence.

Kenojuak was expecting her second child, and with the help of Kingwatsiak's wife and her sister-in-law, Elisapee, she gave birth to her daughter, Mary.

The year 1950 harboured major changes for Sikusiilaq. Other nations were starting to show an interest in the Arctic's natural resources. For reasons of political expediency, the Canadian government considered it a matter of urgency to show a presence in the Arctic regions. As part of the program, a teacher and a nurse were for the first time sent to Cape Dorset – A. F. 'Bill' Applewhite and his wife Phyllis. This was the beginning of general school education for the young Inuit and from now on, the inhabitants of the community and the surrounding camps had permanent access to medical aid.

In his book, Peter Pitseolak has provided some background information on this latest development.[15] Among those on board the ill-fated *Nascopie* and who came to Cape Dorset after the ship sank were two government officials charged with responsibility for health and education in the Inuit settlements. They asked Pitseolak whether he considered it desirable to have teachers and nurses sent to Cape Dorset. He was the 'boss' there, so it was up to him to decide.

When Pitseolak expressed his approval, the officials asked for two men to act as witnesses. Pitseolak chose his brother Pootoogook as one of the witnesses. The latter raised the understandable question why Pitseolak should see himself as the boss, since he, Pootoogook, was by far the elder of the two. Pitseolak tells that his answer was, "Age has nothing to do with it. I was picked to be the boss."

This argument between the two brothers inspired Pootoogook to demonstrate his power and authority more openly from then on. Although Peter Pitseolak was the undisputed leader in his own camp, Kiattuq, Pootoogook succeeded, with the help of his sons, in expanding his sphere of influence over the entire southern part of Baffin Island to Iqaluit; he is remembered as the 'Eskimo King.' People today have told us, referring to the rivalry between the two brothers, that "Peter Pitseolak wanted to be a great leader; Pootoogook *was* a great leader."

The Applewhites spent two years in Cape Dorset, and when their assignment came to an end, they found it very difficult to part. Applewhite has put down in writing the things that happened during that time.[16]

Iceberg before Dorset Island (July 1996)

Cape Dorset: the Kuugalaak part of the community,
referred to as 'the Valley'

Cape Dorset: 'the Valley'

Cape Dorset Cemetery and the Anglican church nestling in 'the Valley'

Johnniebo's grave, bearing the inscription
'Janivvu Asivaq | 1923 | 08.09.72'

Caribou antlers; view across to the neighbouring island of Mallikjuak

An afternoon swim in mid-June –
the temperature of the air and water: 6°C

Cape Dorset, with Kinngait in the background

Kenojuak's home since 1979 in the Itjurittuq part of Cape Dorset

Kenojuak and her 'National Aboriginal Achievement Award'

'Companion to the Order of Canada'

A narrator full of temperament

A proud grandmother with a daughter of Pudlo
and Adamie's adopted son, Towkie

Happy about an Arctic char prepared for drying

Friends for many years: Kenojuak and Jimmy Manning

A chance encounter after doing the shopping

A. F. 'Bill' Applewhite was a man whose life had taken many unusual turns, even for a Canadian. For twelve long years he had stuck it out at a school in Ontario, in the small community of Oakland, near Brantford, before the daily routine became too monotonous for him to bear. He wanted to do something totally different, possibly even missionary work. Several offers were made, but one attracted him especially – the authorities were looking for a married couple who could work in the health and education field in remote areas of Canada, in the far North, for example. As an experienced teacher, and his wife Phyllis a trained nurse, they seemed ideally suited to the task, and so in early 1950 they accepted a posting to Cape Dorset. They had never heard the name of the settlement in their lives before and had not the slightest notion of where it might be.

Nevertheless, that summer in Winnipeg they boarded a train bound for Churchill on Hudson Bay, and from there travelled onwards aboard the *C. D. Howe* to the southwest coast of Baffin Island. It was a stormy passage; the ship was flung about like a cork on the violent sea, and Applewhite was so seasick he wished he could die.

The *C. D. Howe* on which the Applewhites travelled to their new place of work was an ice-breaker fitted with the necessary medical and technical equipment to serve as a hospital ship. At the same time it would transport patients, who had to undergo medical treatment away from home und could withstand the journey, down South. Vice versa, those who had recovered were taken back to their Arctic homes. Most of the patients were people who had caught tuberculosis, who were first taken to the Parc Savard Hospital, near Montreal, or to a specialized clinic in Quebec. Many were later sent to a sanatorium in Hamilton. The patients usually spent months or even years far from their relatives. The mortality rate was very high, and quite a number died without ever seeing their homeland again – for many, departure for the South was their last farewell.

At virtually the same time as the *C. D. Howe* and the Applewhites, the supply ship made its annual call, bringing with it a consignment of building materials that were simply unloaded onto the beach. The bulk consisted mainly of pre-fabricated components for houses, made in Montreal by a company called 'Tower Construction.' Local residents and Inuit people from the nearby camps, including Johnniebo, who came over from Saatturittuq, put together under no real expert guidance the first school house and next to it a small building that would be the teacher's home. This house was anything but luxurious; it was a flat-roofed building in the 'matchbox' style commonplace in the Arctic settlements, and consisted of nothing more than two bedrooms and a place to cook. Even though the school building was simple in construction, too, it fulfilled the standards required in the North those days, accommodating as many as fifty or sixty schoolchildren. It had oil-fired heaters and electric light, but the latter did not always operate the way Applewhite might have wished.

Applewhite had only the vaguest of ideas what he was letting himself in for. He knew from twelve years' experience, of course, how best to approach young people in his capacity as teacher. He also knew the curricula that generally applied throughout the South. When he and his wife landed in Cape Dorset, they were mentally prepared for unexpected situations that would confront them. But all that was of little use to them, for the simple reason that the Inuit did not speak English and, worse still, they understood not a single word.

In general, the people in Cape Dorset were so kind and hospitable that Applewhite gladly accentuated that these were probably the finest people he had met in his whole life. As an especially leading personality Applewhite got to know Pootoogook in those early days, and his brother Peter Pitseolak struck him as an intelligent man with a wealth of experience as well.

In his opinion, the Inuit are 'religious' in the best sense of the word, making every endeavour to lead good lives and adhere strictly to the teachings in the Bible. However, he also notes that most of them tend to be superstitious and still believe in spirits.

He communicated with them with a variety of gestures, winks of the eye and a mixture of English and Inuktitut words. Still, he was not satisfied with a situation in which he was unable to converse normally with the inhabitants of the settlement. In order to write the reports he had to submit each month, he was forced to rely on indirect sources of information; sometimes, as a result, he came to absurd conclusions that he himself could only shake his head at years later. For example, in a report on sanitary conditions he once wrote if people here had water to make tea, they also had water to bathe in. Later, he commented ironically, "I don't know if you've ever tried it, but it is difficult to have a bath in an igloo. It is really cold when certain parts of the anatomy touch the snow walls...." As a consequence, Peter Pitseolak used the bath tubs from the *Nascopie* as a place to cut up seals; in any case, he had no inclination to take a bath.

The former warehouse of the Baffin Trading Company, which had been left unused for two years, was now to become the nursing station. The material needed for converting the building and the other medical items required by the following summer had arrived at the same time as had the two newcomers. But Applewhite, who was not exactly a carpenter by trade, was now confronted with the task of designing and constructing a nursing station. It started to be used even while the building work was still in process because too many people in the settlement or from camps in the immediate neighbourhood and beyond were suffering from various diseases and had been hoping for medical aid for too long. Tuberculosis, in particular, was rampant, and many people with the disease had already resigned themselves to their fate and were waiting for slow, sure death.

However, there was one problem concerning the nursing station with which nobody had reckoned – the former warehouse of the Baffin Trading Company was haunted by the ghost of Felix Conrad, the unfortunate manager who had died here of methanol intoxication four years previously. In any case, the Inuit were firmly convinced of the fact and tried to convince Applewhite of the same, because of the awe and fear they felt especially during darkness, if ever they dared to set foot in the building. One day, as Applewhite was leaving the school, he heard loud screaming from the direction of the nursing station. Thinking that Kuyu, the woman who did all the odd jobs there, had hurt her arm in the wringer washing machine, he rushed into the building and found her sitting there, her face as white as chalk. All he could get out of her was that there was a *qallunaaq* with a dog on the upper floor; the rest he failed to understand. It was not until later in the evening, when Tommy Manning came to interpret, that he discovered what had happened. Apparently, Kuyu's little daughter, who was in the nursing station with her mother, had looked up the stairs and seen a white man with a dog – she stood petrified, unable to move. The child's cry had alarmed the mother, who came looking to see; when she grabbed the little girl and looked up the stairs herself, she saw the ghost as well. Nothing could talk her out of thinking she had seen the ghost of Felix Conrad; for days on end she shivered with horror whenever her thoughts turned to the event. After that incident, none of the Inuit was keen on being seen in the staircase of the nursing station.

Phyllis Applewhite worked day and night as a nurse, and the teacher at her side played a part, too, in looking after the health of those entrusted to their care, which sometimes involved emergencies of one kind or another. At the same time, they both tried to adapt their own lives to conditions in the North and to cope with their own everyday problems.

Almost as a sideline, Applewhite strove to discharge his primary responsibilities and provide school education to a class of six to eight Inuit children. An adequate supply of books and other teaching materials were at his disposal. Some things could be managed by simple means, but his attempts to teach the children English met with little success. They seemed to take an almost stubborn attitude when asked to say something in English or to learn English words. Applewhite thinks it would be wrong to say that his pupils had no interest in the subject, the problem was that they obviously saw no purpose whatsoever in learning English, so they made little progress. In the end, he had a better command of Inuktitut than they had of English.

As a teacher, of course, Applewhite was interested in the methods by which the Inuit educated their children. The *qallunaat* thought they could teach children discipline and proper conduct with corporal punishment, by 'slapping the backside,' for example, but among the Inuit such practices are anything but commonplace. They scolded their children and made them feel ridiculous when they did something wrong. Ridicule was about the worst thing in the world for young Inuit, and so they quickly learned how to behave.

Somewhat bemused, Applewhite tells about how he had among other things certain public administration duties to discharge in his capacity as a teacher. He found it ridiculous, if not debasing, to have to monitor closely how hunters or trappers went shopping for food and how they spent their money in general; the government authorities in the South considered it particularly important that the welfare benefit they provided should be spent on wholesome food and quality children's clothing, but they failed to realize that hunting, which was still vitally necessary for families here, was only possible if the hunter himself had the right means at his disposal, including hunting weapons and ammunition.

Already in those days, wireless communication with the outside world by radio amateurs played a key role. The manager of the Hudson's Bay trading post had a 25-watt transmitter-receiver, for example, with which he could contact the station in Charlottetown on Prince Edward Island when atmospheric conditions were right. There was a better radio link between the latter station and Pangnirtung, where the next doctor was; Charlottetown in the South thus became a relay station. The nurse often used this opportunity to obtain advice regarding diagnosis and treatment of diseases, the symptoms of which she described in detail to the doctor on the other end of the line.

To top it all, the South Baffin region suffered the misfortune of a severe measles epidemic in the spring of 1952. The Inuit had no immunological resistance against this imported disease. People ran high temperatures and their skin went deep red donning the appearance of dark velvet. Some of those on the way to recovery left their beds too early had a relapse and eventually died of pneumonia. In Cape Dorset alone, fourteen people died of the latter illness. Tending to the sick night and day was an extreme challenge, not only for the Applewhites, but also for the Catholic missionary, Father Lemaire, the employees of the Hudson's Bay Company, and not least the Inuit who managed to stay healthy.

Penicillin was then available for the very first time, and had to be injected at intervals of 36 or 72 hours. The necessary needles had to be used again and again, so they had to be cleaned and sterilized every time. Applewhite tells of how he, the school teacher, had to find out the right size of needle for each injection and the right dose to give. He goes on to say that he has been certainly not the 'best injection giver of the world,' and that some of the Inuit would certainly confirm this.

When more and more people fell ill and could no longer be cared for in the nursing station, the Applewhites were compelled to convert the school building into a hospital. The Canadian Air Force flew emergency missions, throwing down essential blankets, as well as additional rations of evaporated milk because the Hudson's Bay Company was running out of stock. During the epidemic, there were always more than thirty patients with measles in the school, and they had to be fed with large amounts of hot soup made from dehydrated vegetables, and, of course, milk and tea.

Kuyu, the 'Girl Friday' in the nursing station, fell ill herself and came very close to death. For three, four days, she lay motionless in bed with high fever. Despite cold baths and medication, Applewhite was unable to bring down her temperature. In his distress, he radioed from the Hudson's Bay post the doctor in Pangnirtung to find out if there was anything else that could possibly be done. Just at that moment, Kuyu's husband came running up, bursting with excitement – Kuyu was standing up in bed, shouting and screaming, and for God's sake, Applewhite should come quickly and help. He found the patient sitting on her bed, thinking her last hour had come. She pleaded with him to bid farewell to all her family and relatives for her. He was convinced then that Kuyu had survived the crisis and would recover, which is how things turned out.

During the time the Applewhites were working in Cape Dorset, a man by the name of James Houston (or 'Saumik,' the left-handed one, as the Inuit soon called him) arrived in the settlement, accompanied by his young wife, Allie (Alma). That was in the spring of 1951. Houston had studied art in Canada and France and, like many before and after him, had been obsessed by the Inuit and their country ever since he had first come to the Arctic (we invented the term 'Arctic virus infection' to explain our own case). On his earlier travels into the Arctic, he had recognized the artistic talents that lay dormant in the Inuit, and was now underway as a 'Northern Service Officer' to offer his assistance to the camp-dwellers along the south coast of Baffin.

Guided by experienced Inuit, the Houstons had travelled more than 450 kilometres by dog sled from Iqaluit (Frobisher Bay); it had been a long and difficult trek that took them first to Kimmirut (Lake Harbour), then farther westwards. On the way, the lack of food for both the people and the sled dogs was a constant source of worry. Their hopes of stocking up with fresh supplies in Camp Qarmaaqjuk were dashed, as were their hopes, when all their reserves were exhausted, of obtaining food in Pootoogook's Camp Ikirasak – Pootoogook and his family were not there. The Houstons then crossed the broad expanse of Andrew Gordon Bay and arrived at Camp Itilliaqjuk, whose leader was Saggiak (the singer of songs that Peter Pitseolak mentioned in his tales of shamanism). This was where Houston first met Osuitok, with whom he has been close friends ever since – but more of that later. Lack of food prevailed in Itilliaqjuk, too; hunting was doomed to failure by the severe weather conditions and the state of the ice. Bannock was all the travellers could be given to eat, and again there was nothing for the dogs. In the last camp on this journey, Kiattuq, Houston became acquainted with Peter Pitseolak, who welcomed the visitors with his special brand of warmth and hospitality; yet here, too, there was no meat to eat, and yet again the dogs had to go without. Summoning the last of their energies, the travellers finally reached Cape Dorset.[17] Over the ten years that followed, Houston was to emphasize substantial points, exerting a fundamental influence on developments in Sikusiilaq.

II

In hospital

The city of Quebec:
Kenojuak's lung disease – homesick for the North

In the summer of 1951, Johnniebo and his family moved to Camp Qarmaaqjuk on Amadjuak Bay. The camp was situated about half-way between the settlements of Kimmirut (Lake Harbour) and Cape Dorset and, as the name suggests, originally comprised a substantial number of *qarmaqs* (sod houses). The Hudson's Bay Company had serviced the wider area from here for a while – especially the island the Inuit call Akudnik (Salisbury Island). According to Peter Pitseolak, people on this island often went hungry and were dependent on support from the Company. The trading post had been abandoned as early as 1934.

 Today, the old timber building of the trading post is rather decayed, but still more or less intact. People still believe it is haunted by ghosts. Even our interpreter, Jeannie Manning, tells us about an experience she herself had:

Around 1962 several of my family and myself stopped at the abandoned trading post heading there in our Peterhead boat. We were going part of the way with some relatives who were travelling to Kimmirut in their own Peterhead boat, and the plan was to stay overnight at the trading post. One of the men tried to open the door to get inside the old building, but he wasn't able to do so. So he shouted to the other men to come and help, but even together they didn't manage to break open the door. In the end they gave up. When I heard from my brother what had happened, I went over and just pushed open the door, quite easily. I then went in and climbed the stairs; I was just a small child – I was about four years old then – and the ghosts didn't put up any resistance.

In that summer of 1951, Kenojuak had to go for another X-ray examination. Some time after, a patrol of the Royal Canadian Mounted Policy (RCMP) came to Camp Qarmaaqjuk on their way from Kimmirut to Cape Dorset and informed her that she had been diagnosed as having tuberculosis. They also gave her to understand that she would have to go for treatment to a hospital in the South the first chance she got – terrible news for the young woman to bear.

Not much later, Kenojuak gave birth to her third child, a boy to whom she gave the name Qiqituk. Since her stay in hospital was imminent, she and Johnniebo thought about what should be done with the newborn child. Johnniebo's mother was already so advanced in years that caring for the baby would have been too much of a burden for her. They decided to let Qiqituk be adopted straight after his birth by Latchaolassie Akesuk and his wife, Kenojuak's cousin Saimaijuk.

Christmas had just passed when the RCMP patrol passed through the camp again on the way back to Kimmirut (Lake Harbour). They wanted Kenojuak to come with them straight away so they could take her to a ship embarking for the South. Johnniebo, however, was in Cape Dorset to barter for food supplies. Therefore she refused point blank to leave with the Mounties, insisting on seeing Johnniebo one more time before leaving. In the end, it was decided that Kenojuak should first travel to Cape Dorset with a few other patients from Camp Qarmaaqjuk, and sail for the South from there.

Before leaving Qarmaaqjuk, Kenojuak gave her two children, Jamasie and Mary, into the care of her mother-in-law, Kadlarjuk. After that Kenojuak and three other tuberculosis patients[18] set off on their long journey by dog sled. The first stage took them to Camp Kallusiqbik on Saqbak Bay – the bay where Kenojuak and Johnniebo had spent a brief period just after they married, until Peter Pitseolak fetched them to Kiattuq. In Camp Kallusiqbik they met

Johnniebo, who was on his way home to Qarmaaqjuk. They had only one night in which to say their farewells before having to part in the morning. Johnniebo knew what lay in store for him, but Kenojuak's future was much less certain. Although she felt frightened and alone, she had no idea that three and a half years were to pass before Johnniebo could embrace her again.

The next stage of the journey took them to Camp Ikirasak, where Kenojuak had been born twenty-five years previously. Here, too, their stay was limited to just one night. The next morning they were joined by more patients – Ponitsak and Josie, whose husband Paulassie Pootoogook now accompanied the travellers to the nursing station in Cape Dorset, where Uttuqi and Pauta Saila's first wife, Matsauzak, were waiting to be transported south.

A few days later they boarded the plane – a completely new experience for Kenojuak and her fellow-travellers – and flew to Iqaluit (Frobisher Bay), then onwards to Goose Bay in Labrador. In the hospital where she stayed the night, Kenojuak met Simonie Michael. He had just returned from England after an audience with the Queen, and was able to act as interpreter for the new arrivals. They only spoke Inuktitut and could not understand a word of English. Simonie also helped them lose a little of their fear.

The next day they were flown to the city of Quebec, where they were taken to hospital. Here they met some patients from Cape Dorset who had been there a while already, such as Ashevak Ezekiel, Salamonie Pootoogook, Mary Qaqjurajuk and a number of children. They were overjoyed to see the newcomers and asked eagerly for news from home. Salamonie never saw his home country ever again; he was later moved to the sanatorium in Hamilton, Ontario, where he passed away.

The hospital building had three storeys and separate wards for men, women and children. They were allowed to visit each other, though, something they greatly enjoyed. Nevertheless, the days were growing longer and longer for Kenojuak. She saw patients coming from all parts of the eastern Arctic for treatment, some of whom remained here until they died. The only link to relatives left behind consisted at best of occasional correspondence, and sometimes new arrivals brought messages from their homes far, far away.

One day, when her stepfather Nuvualia also arrived for treatment, Kenojuak learned from him that her grandfather Alariaq had died after protracted illness. Hardly anybody from Cape Dorset came to see her. Two exceptions were James and Alma Houston, who occasionally dropped in on her and told her what was going on back home; they did not know each other too well yet in those days because Kenojuak had been taken to Quebec not long after their arrival at Cape Dorset.

Many of the patients spent months and years far away from their families, and so the hospital management tried to give them something meaningful to do. This was one of the reasons why the Houstons came here so frequently. The main purpose of their visits was to supply the patients with materials for artwork. Kenojuak also received drawing paper, we are told by James Houston, but none of her work from those days is still in existence, and Kenojuak herself can no longer remember any details.

In the late fall of 1953 – Kenojuak had been undergoing clinical treatment for a year and a half by now – Salamonie Pootoogook received a letter from his parents containing terrible news for her. Kenojuak's two children were no longer alive. During late spring Jamasie had died of trichinosis after eating walrus meat infested with trichina. He was not the only victim; other people in the camp died with him, including three of Tikituk's and Lucy's children. Johnniebo, too, had been infected, but he managed to survive the dreadful disease. Late that summer, when the supply ship that came every year had already left the Sikusiilaq area, her daughter Mary fell sick as well, and died in the Cape Dorset nursing station. The two children were buried near Camp Kiattuuq.

One day, Kenojuak received a long letter from Johnniebo, imploring her not to grieve too much over the loss of their two children. She should concentrate instead on her own health and recovery so that she could return to Cape Dorset as soon as possible. Despite Johnniebo's letter, Kenojuak was close to collapse. She suffered unbearably from these agonizing events and seriously considered having no more children. The Inuit in the hospital prayed for her. She herself confesses to us that praying was the only way to keep her going. "When I was told my children had died, I felt totally abandoned. My husband and I had to go through so much without being able to console each other."

During our conversations, Kenojuaks's deep religious feelings made a strong impression on us again and again. What does she think awaits her after death? "I wish to go to heaven. I believe I will be reunited there with my father, my mother, my husband and with all those I love. Nobody can know what the future will bring – God will know, but I hope to go to heaven." Her grandmother, Quitsaq, had become acquainted with Christianity while in the far north of Quebec. She had a prayer book that was printed in Inuktitut with syllabic symbols; an Anglican missionary had left it to her.

At an early age, Kenojuak had started learning syllabics and reading the prayer book, the only printed matter in the family. This was how she learned to read and write in her mother tongue, despite never going to school.[*]

In the camps on Baffin Island, Kenojuak saw missionaries on rare occasions only. The *Nascopie*, however, almost always had a priest on board whose mission was to visit the settlements, christening children, wedding couples who had been married the customary way, or explaining passages in the Bible so that the people could follow the church services.

While she was mentally already preparing herself for her discharge from hospital and returning home, Kenojuak suffered a dangerous relapse; she found out later that she had contracted non-tubercular pneumonia. Her severe coughing fits and spitting of blood were great cause for concern; she could not move about and had difficulty breathing. For these reasons she was transferred to the 'hopeless cases ward.'

When lying there so gravely ill, Kenojuak had a powerful dream. She saw an enormous building with many entrances; inside it, she could see her children in

---

[*] The system of phonetic writing of Inuktitut using syllabics (see pp. 116 - 117) was introduced to the Inuit of the eastern Arctic by missionaries from 1876 onwards, most notably by Edmund J. Peck (symbols of this kind were originally used by the Cree Indians). Long before schools were founded in the eastern Arctic, about 90 percent of the Inuit were able to read and write Inuktitut by means of syllabics. Recent decades have seen growth in phonetic writing using Latin characters as well.

the company of other children and adolescents. She also recognized a friend's sister who had died in the hospital. In one of the rooms stood a group of excited people. Her father, garbed in a magnificent white robe, had taken a seat high up on a ladder. A huge accordion hung above him. Kenojuak tried to touch him, but he pulled away from her and conveyed to her that she could not go to him until her mother, Silaqqi, was by his side. In that moment, Kenojuak had the feeling as if she were about to lose her soul. She woke up, and the worst was over. Kenojuak has been firmly convinced ever since that her life was saved through the influence of her father.

It took some time before she could stand on her legs and walk again, but she gradually recovered her strength. In the end, she was allowed to go back to the normal ward and the friends she had there. Peter Pitseolak had also arrived in the meantime; it was 1957 before he was let out again.

Inuktitut syllabics

116

ᐱᐅᒋᑐᓕᕙ ᐃᓂᒧ, ᔨᓯᓯᒧ ᑕᒪᐳ. ᑕᓂᒐ, ᔨᓯᓯᑉ ᐃᓄᓕᔭ, ᑯᕕᒋᓂᒧ ᐃᓂᐊᒍᓴᑐᑐ-ᐃᓕᓗᒍ...ᑎᒥᒥᓂ ᐸᒉᑕᓴᓯᓗᒍ,ᓇᒪᑎᓯᓂ-ᒧ ᐃᓇᒍᑎᓗᒍ...ᐱᐅᒋᓂᐃᔭᓂᑯ ᒪᑭᑎᓗᒍ...ᐃᓗᐊᓴᑲᑕᓗᒍ ᐱᒪᒍ ᐊᓯᒍᐅ ᑕᓂᒐ ᔨᓯᓯᑉ ᐃᓕᒋᓗᐊᐸ...ᑕᒉᓂ ᐃᑲᕙᑎᐊᓗᒍ...ᑯᕕ-ᐊᓇᑐᕕᒧ ᑐᒐᐅᓯᑯᒋᓗᒐ...ᓯᓇᐅᕙᓕ, ᐅᕙᒐ...ᐃᓚᓂ... ᑎᒥᒪ ᐃᓄᓯᐊ ᑲᒪᒋᔭᑐᐊᒐ...ᑐᑯᕕᒪ ᐅᒐᑕᓂ...ᐱᑲᑕᓂ ᓄᒍᓯᐃᑐᒥ ᑲ ᐃᓄᓯᑲᒐᔭᒋᑐᒐ;ᑌᒪᓇ ᑐᑭ ᑲᑐᐅᔭᑲᑕᒐᒪ...ᐃᓚᓂ,ᐅᐱᒋᑐᑐ ᐃᓕ-ᑯᓯᑲᓗᒐ...ᑯᔭᓇ-ᐊᑐᐃᓇᓗᒐᓗ...ᐃᓯᒪᓯᒍᐊᓗᒐᓗ ᐱᕙᑲᒪ ... ᑕᓂᒪ ᐃᓄᓯᐊ ᑯᔭᓇ-ᐊᒍᑎᓴᐅᒋᒪ;ᑕᓂᒐ ᓯᓗᑕᓂ ᐃᓕᒍᓯᓇᓂᓴᐅᒪ ᓯᓇᓗᑕᓂ ᔨᓯᓯᑉ ᐊᓂᒋᒪᒍ...ᐊᐅᒥᓄ ᐊᑭᓕᓚᐅᓗᒍ ᓇᒥᓂᒋᓇᓯᑲ-ᒥᐅ.

ᑎᒥᒐ...ᐊᓂᐊᓇᑐᒧᓗᕙ...ᑐᑯᓇᑐᒧᓗᕙ ᐱᔭᐅᑌᓕᓕᑯᓗᒍ.. ᐅᔮᑐᐸᑕᒐᓗᐊᒐ. ᑕᓂᒐᓗᑕᐅ ᑌᒪᓇᐃᓕᐅᒥᓚᒍ...ᐱᐅᒋᑐᓕᓂ ᒪᒥ-ᐊᓇᑐᐅᒪ...ᐱᐅᒋᑐᓕᓕᒐᒐᒪ...ᐱᐅᒋᑐᒧ ᐃᓚᒋᐅᑎᑲᒪ... ᐃᓚ ᑕᓂᒐ, ᔨᓯᓯᑉ ᐃᓕᒋᔭ,ᓯᑐᐃᓇᓂ ᐊᑭᑐᓂᓴᐅᕗ...ᐊᐅᒥᓄ ᐱᓯᐊ-ᒋᒪᒍ...ᐱᐅᒋᑐᓕᑎᓗᒐ, ᓴᑐᐃᒐᒪ ᑕᓂᒻᓂᒃ...ᑲᐱᐊᓇᑐᕕᐅ ᐸ ᐃᓄᐊᓄ ᐱᔭᐅᑯᓗᒍ,ᐱᕙᑎᑲᓗᒐ ᔨᓯᓯᑉ ᐃᓗᐊᒋᒋᑕᓂ ᐱᑯᒋᑕᓂ... ᓄᒍᐊᓚᕙᒥ...ᓯᓇᐅᒋᑐᒥ...ᐃᓯᒪᐃᑐᑐ-ᐃᓕᒐᒐᒪ ᑕᕙ.

A syllabic prayer-book text in Inuktitut

Harold Pfeiffer, the sculptor, paid almost daily visits to the hospital from fall 1954 onwards. He was the brother of Kenojuak's doctor, Walter Pfeiffer, and saw to those patients who were involved in arts and crafts. He helped them not only to spend their time in hospital in meaningful ways, but also to earn some 'pocket money' in the process. The hospital was willing to sell the finished works of art and craft articles on behalf of the patients. Harold Pfeiffer brought his 'students' materials with which they were unfamiliar and inspired them to experiment. If patients did not have to stay in bed, they got involved in beadwork, sewing, leatherwork and above all wood carving.

Kenojuak never tried her hand at the latter although some of the men showed her how to do it. However, she enjoyed attending Pfeiffer's art classes. Her teacher was very impressed with the dolls she made out of textile and leather remnants. "They are some of the best and most beautiful I have ever seen," was his assessment. The figures were dressed in traditional costumes, wore white cotton parkas with decorative beadwork and soft leather *kamiks* and mittens, all sewn together with the finest of stitching. Kenojuak used a template card to cut out the parkas. As Pfeiffer confirmed, using a template and designing cut-out patterns was Kenojuak's own idea; he just supplied her with material and showed her the work of other patients as well as various magazine illustrations.

One day in May 1955, Harold Pfeiffer's brother Walter, her doctor, came into her room and gaily announced that she finally would be allowed to go home within the next few weeks. He also had a pleasant surprise for Kenojuak – before they embarked on the *C. D. Howe* in late June, he took his recuperated patients on a sightseeing tour. For the first time in her life, Kenojuak went to a zoo and became acquainted with Quebec and the surrounding countryside. She also visited the grave of one of Tikituk's and Lucy's sons, who had not survived the disease. He was the fourth child that the couple had lost within a short period, as three others had died of trichinosis. Walter Pfeiffer went a step farther, taking his newly-recovered patients to his home and showing them his fantastic collection of art. Kenojuak was deeply impressed by the trip. She tells us that her first ever encounter with modern European art was on that day. For example she saw sculptures by Henry Moore that pleased her immensely.

Harold Pfeiffer was also on board the *C. D. Howe* and accompanied the recuperated on their journey up north. On the ship, Kenojuak became friends with Sarah Ikummiaq, who was working as the ship's interpreter. The weather was very stormy during the crossing, and many passengers were tormented by seasickness. But when the repatriates saw the first drift ice, all the rigours of the journey were forgotten; they felt rejuvenated because their homeland was welcoming them back. There was a rough sea as the ship reached Kimmirut (Lake Harbour), the first port of call. Kenojuak was overwhelmed to see again the familiar coastline of Baffin Island. She was ferried to shore, where she saw her mother among the waiting crowd. Silaqqi had received word that Kenojuak was coming home at last on board the ship, and could not rest. She had hurried to Kimmirut with her son Adamie, in order to accompany her daughter to Cape Dorset.

Kenojuak had a sad duty to perform first, however, and handed over to her mother the personal belongings of Nuvualia, her third husband; he, too, had been snatched away by that malicious disease, tuberculosis, while in hospital. Having done so she set to gorging herself on the seal meat that her relatives had brought with them and which she had been missing for so long.

When the *C. D. Howe* finally arrived in Cape Dorset, Johnniebo was waiting among the crowd on the shore. Kenojuak realized just how much she missed her children at that very happy moment of her return. The two of them stayed in Cape Dorset for a couple of days while Johnniebo helped unload the ship. Accompanied by Tikituk and Lucy, they then set out for Camp Kangiaq, where almost all their relatives were now living.

III

Back in camps

Kangiaq and Kiattuuq:
Working as an artist

Camp Kangiaq was located amidst great hunting grounds. When Kenojuak arrived, the fox-trapping season was about to start, and Johnniebo, Tikituk and Niviaqsi tackled the job of preparing the traps. Compared to previous years, however, the situation they were now facing was completely different. The value of fox furs had plummeted, and the price paid that fall of 1955 was much less than before. Setting traps no longer generated an adequate level of income, and the people in the camp began to worry about what to expect that winter. As much as she was looking forward to fishing, it was now more important for Kenojuak to re-acquire all those previous skills that she had more or less lost while hospitalized – her daily routines and the dexterity required by camp life, especially the processing of animal skins. Towkie's wife Elisapee was a help in this respect.

In the days when she was still living with her grandmother, the typical chores of a woman included making clothes the traditional way from animal skins and furs. Kenojuak had raised this to a technical skill of great artistry. Even when she was a young girl, the women in camp would approach her about her highly artistic *kamiks* (boots made from animal skins and furs). Yet she had always refused to make leather articles for others.

In order to obtain different shadings of colour, the animal skins were tanned by a variety of methods. By scraping off or cutting the hairs, it was possible to enhance the desired effects. Shading and colour effects were achieved on seal skins by shearing the hair in different lengths. Another technique involved sewing leather cut-outs onto the actual item of clothing or inserting them into recesses; wall hangings and skin bags were decorated the same way.

Wool and cotton had been introduced to the Arctic regions by whalers, researchers and missionaries not later than the turn of the century, and were therefore known in Quitsaq's camp as well. When the Hudson's Bay Company established its trading posts, the Inuit women were able to obtain all kinds of sewing articles. It did not take long before intricate embellishments were added to needlework products using gaily-coloured threads of wool and glass beads; the embroidery materials imported from the South had inspired the women's imagination.

Inuit clothing was very popular with visitors to the Arctic and sold quickly. They were worn not only in the north for their intended purpose; more importantly they were also taken back home down south by their proud owners as souvenirs, making Inuit culture better known in other regions. Over the years, as transportation to the Arctic continuously improved, a growing market developed for Inuit craftwork, especially *kamiks*, mittens and parkas. Sealskin carrier bags and wall hangings as well as artistic dolls made from a variety of materials were manufactured by the women for sale and decorated with beadwork or traditional designs.

Soon after his arrival at Cape Dorset in the early 1950s, James Houston gave the men various kinds of tasks to accomplish so that they could acquire at least a certain degree of economic independence. Under his guidance they began to produce stone carvings and later learned how to prepare and print graphic art. Houston's wife Alma, called Arnakotak ('the tall-grown lady') by the Inuit, got involved in the various projects of the women in the settlement. She focused her energy, her enthusiasm, her time, her skills and her knowledge on making sure the women were also able to contribute towards supporting their families by selling their arts and crafts.

The starting point for the Houstons' efforts lay in the fact that the Inuit had a long-standing tradition in the art of stone carving and in the ornamentation of everyday utility objects made of other materials. What could be more natural than to exploit these traditional skills in order to improve the economic situation? As a result, an art centre for stone carving and prints developed in Cape Dorset. Sales were initially organized by the only commercial enterprise in the community, the Hudson's Bay Company, before it was superseded by a new marketing organization run by the Inuit themselves. But it was a long and laborious process before things developed so far.

At first, the situation in Cape Dorset bore similarities to that in the northern part of Quebec. There, only the men carved sculptures in stone, with but occasional support from the women and children in polishing the surface. The women added to their income by sewing and weaving baskets. However, it was not long before the women, too, turned their hand to the art of stone carving (although the men did not follow suit and start sewing).

Early on in the 1950s, the art and craft objects for sale were still very traditional as far as style and production techniques were concerned. This was to change in the second half of the decade. The project to create special 'Inuit prints' was influenced by totally new elements and first got started in early winter 1957 in Cape Dorset. James Houston has described this phase in considerable detail.[19]

The technique of using paper drawings as a basis for subsequent stone cuttings and etchings was already applied in some of the first prints. But first and foremost, there were the highly contrastive and powerful decorative work on hand-made caribou and seal skin bags, and the traditional patterns on ivory objects that offered themselves to be transformed into graphic art.

Qiatsuq and Kenojuak's uncle Niviaqsi had been drawing pictures long before the Houstons' arrival on the scene; they may have been encouraged by researchers working previously in the Cape Dorset area, such as J. Dewey Soper, the scientist and painter. In any case, it was by no means unusual in the first half of the century for visitors to be asking the Inuit for drawings, and, indeed, Inuit experts like Robert Flaherty and Knud Rasmussen collected some excellent works of art. Houston himself says he was very struck by Qiatsuq and Niviaqsi's drawings, and showed them some of his own sketches. Even at that time there was one man in particular who displayed exceptional interest in the artistic developments, a man who was soon to rank highly among the Inuit artists. His name was Osuitok. Houston had first met him years before in Camp Itilliaqjuk, and the two often sat together. Houston describes the course that developments took as follows:[20]

Osuitok sat near me one evening casually studying the sailor's head to be seen as a trademark on two identical packages of cigarettes ['Player's Navy Cut']. He noted carefully every subtle detail of color and form, then stated that it must have been very tiresome for some artist to sit painting every one of the little heads on the packages with the exact sameness.

I tried to explain this in Inuktitut, as best I could, about 'civilized' man's technical progress in the field of printing little packages, which involved the entire offset color printing process. My explanation was far from successful, partly because of my inability to find the right words to describe terms such as 'intaglio' and 'color register', and partly because I was starting to wonder whether this could have any practical application in Inuit terms.

Looking around to find some way to demonstrate printing, I saw an ivory tusk that Osuitok had recently engraved. The curved tusk was about fifteen inches long. Osuitok had carefully smoothed and polished it and had incised bold engravings on both sides. Into the lines of these engravings he had rubbed black soot gathered from his family's seal-oil lamp.

Taking an old tin of writing ink that had frozen and thawed many times, with my finger I dipped up the black residue and smoothed it over the tusk. Then taking a thin piece of toilet tissue, I laid it on the inked surface and rubbed the top lightly, then quickly stripped the paper from the tusk. I saw that by mere good fortune, I had pulled a fairly good negative image of Osuitok's incised design.

"We could do that," he said, with the instant decision of a hunter. And so we did.

Certainly the Inuit had pictorial illustrations based on ancient traditions and myths; and, on the whole, they also possessed extraordinary dexterity and a well-developed sense for technical contexts and possibilities. Printing techniques, however, were unknown to them. Houston succeeded in capturing the interest of four young men – Kananginak, Iyola, Lukta, and Igyvadluk – in the printing project, and they launched into several long series of experiments with stone prints, including the use of stencils.

Among other things, flat reliefs engraved in stone served as printing blocks, albeit with varying success. Houston recalls that "Printing ink was not available, so we tried making ink by mixing seal oil and lamp black. It was awful. We tried schoolchildren's poster paints with better luck. Since there was only one official mail a year, at shiptime, government correspondence was not a large feature of my life, so I borrowed almost all of the official supply of government onionskin stationery, which proved to be excellent for proofing prints." [21]

They soon discovered steatite or serpentine to be the most suitable for working with inks. This mineral, called serpentine because of its green colour, occurs in abundance on western Baffin Island. In those days, it was mainly obtained on Markham Bay, 300 kilometres east of Cape Dorset; today, it is predominantly quarried at Korok Inlet, which is closer. It is fine-grained, relatively soft, but not too porous and for that reason, as good as the best marble for sculpting and carving; on the other hand, it is hard enough for fine polishing. Far back in time, the Inuit had already collected this stone from the quarry during the summer and used it as material for making *qulliqs* and stone pots. One benefit was that the stone cleaved away in large, flat, fist-thick slabs from the rock face, obviating the need to break pieces off.

Kenojuak

Timmun's Beach House, the teacher's house
built in 1950 and converted several times since

A cheerful atmosphere for interviews in the Beach House
(from left to right: Jeannie Manning, Kenojuak, the author)

Ever-changing light conditions: ships in the ice before the
Beach House shine awhiles in the glistening light, before ...

... being coated anew in snow crystals, the whorls of which the sun can only penetrate milky-white. Mallikjuak loses its contours.

The former school building, dating from 1950,
today the 'Natsiq Sewing Centre'

Cape Dorset: the health centre

Cape Dorset in early spring

Our kind hosts in 1995: Adamie and his wife, Ooloosie

Kenojuak's son Adamie, stone carving

Artist working on a stone sculpture

Administration office and printshop building
of the West Baffin Eskimo Co-operative

– and the printshop interior

Kenojuak's adopted son Arnaguq working in the printshop

A printmaker's hands, working on slate with a stencil

A short cigarette break to relax

Slabs like this were less suitable for large sculptures, but all the better as printing blocks. The surface just had to be evened out and polished, then relief drawings could be cut into them, the basis for printing. The technique for transferring the image was quite simple. The smoothed and polished surface of the stone was coated with white latex. The drawing to be printed was then traced onto a sheet of paper. The copy thus obtained was transferred in reverse to the white surface of the stone by using carbon paper, and the resulting picture touched up with drawing ink. The stone cutter now dug into the stone along the lines of the drawing, thus creating an engraved relief. The surface was now ready for inking; black ink or paints were applied to the remaining, raised surface using an ink roller, in accordance with the colours in the original drawing. Once the stone slab had been treated in this way, a suitable sheet of printing paper was placed on it, covered in turn by a second sheet of protective paper, mostly tissue. Finally, the two paper sheets were hand-rubbed onto the dyed slab or with a round seal-skin bale. This was sufficient to transfer the image. First the protective tissue and then the printed sheet were carefully drawn off and the latter hung up to dry.

It was crucial for the print project to meet everyone's acceptance among the Inuit. To this end, James Houston sought the support of the two most important elders in Sikusiilaq – Pootoogook and Qiatsuq:[22] "I got up my nerve and went and asked Pootoogook to make me an illustration of something he had been trying to explain to me. He did this and sent the results next morning. I asked his son, Kananginak, to help print his father's drawing of two caribou. Kananginak gladly did this, assisted by Eegivudluk [Igyvadluk] and other relatives. Pootoogook greatly admired the result, and after that the whole stone block and stencil printing project was off to a powerful start."

In those early days, there were quite a few other problems that also had to be solved. However, these problems were not artistic but primarily technical in nature. For example, it was necessary to find a small building that could be heated where the artists could work and make limited edition prints using the stone block technique. Furthermore, it seemed impossible at first to keep white paper clean – fingerprints got everywhere. Overnight, the ink would thicken from the cold, making it almost impossible to apply it evenly in the morning. "But far more important, we always had the skills, patience, and basic Inuit good nature to carry us through." [23]

Johnniebo and Kenojuak had little to do with these developments at first. They were living in Camp Kangiaq and travelled to Cape Dorset for Christmas 1956. The celebration of this religious feast has ranked high among the Inuit for a long time. When they broke their journey at Peter Pitseolak's Camp Kiattuuq, they learned that the inhabitants had little hunting success for some considerable time and that life was very hard for them. Perhaps worst of all was that they had no seal oil to fuel the *qulliqs* used for heating and cooking (the Coleman stoves that are used everywhere today were not yet available in those days). Living conditions had deteriorated to such an extent that Aggeak Petaulassie and his wife Sheorak urged them to adopt their little boy, just one month old. He should not be growing up in an unheated, cold and damp *qarmaq*. Kenojuak was very happy about the idea, especially since she had been longing for another child again. She named him Arnaguq and could hardly wait to take the baby with them on the way back to Camp Kangiaq.

At the festivities in Kinngait (Cape Dorset), they met various friends and relatives. Games of skill, dog sled races and other contests were held as usual. The evenings were spent in the school building, marvelling at the drum dancers and listening to the throat singing. The latter was a kind of competition in which at least two people (mostly women) produced almost aphonic sounds from their throats in various pitches and rhythms until one of them fell into a fit of laughter and had to stop. The people attending the celebrations enjoyed dancing a lot, to the tune of an accordion played by Aggeok, Peter Pitseolak's wife. Holding the service were Pootoogook and Kingwatsiak, who, for an Inuk, had gotten around a great deal and was now playing a leading role in the settlement.

On the way back, Kenojuak had to borrow a warm sealskin *amautiq* in Camp Kiattuuq so that she could take her adopted son Arnaguq with her. An amautiq is a common outer garment worn by women and has a hood with a special pouch to carry small children in. As they journeyed on towards Kangiaq, they stopped off in Camp Itilliaqjuk, where they were put up in Latchaolassie Akesuk's *qarmaq*. His little son Qiqituk, to whom Kenojuak had given birth shortly before her stay in hospital and then given up for adoption, had died during the measles epidemic that 'Bill' Applewhite has written about.

When Arnaguq was about one year old, Johnniebo's mother, Kadlarjuk, died of old age after a turbulent life of hardship yet also fulfilment; people say that she was more than eighty years old, a very old age for the Inuit. To Kenojuak she bequeathed her *qulliq*, which she had used since the birth of her daughter Aggeok and had taken along everywhere.

In Camp Kangiaq Johnniebo and Kenojuak spent two years before Peter Pitseolak returned from the South after three years in hospital. Again, he called on the two of them to live in his camp, Camp Kiattuuq. In that fall of 1957, when the land was already beginning to freeze over, Kenojuak gave birth to another boy, called Kadlarjuk after Johnniebo's mother. Arnaguq was still too small to walk and kept his mother very busy. Peter Pitseolak, Johnniebo and Kenojuak therefore agreed to give the newborn baby to Abraham Etungat and his wife Etyguyakjuaq for adoption. While waiting for Etungat to come and take the child, Kenojuak cared for and nursed the little one herself. She was heartbroken at having to give away the child, but she had no other choice. The child died only a few months later.

Since their new camp was not so far away, Johnniebo and Kenojuak used to go into Cape Dorset more often now to obtain everyday supplies. They also began to develop an interest and take part in the projects organized by the Houstons. When we talk with her about this period in her life, Kenojuak tells us that she had already begun making artistic work such as cut-outs from seal skin long before James and Alma Houston came to Cape Dorset. Probably as early as 1950 she had made a bag with a shoulder strap, for example. The latter has meanwhile become famous, but has unfortunately been lost. The artwork on it formed the basis for Kenojuak's first ever print, made in 1958 and bearing the title 'Rabbit Eating Seaweed.' But now, with guidance from the Houstons, Kenojuak occupied herself more intensively with such work; she even made her first attempts at carving stone sculptures. Above all, she began making highly artistic seal skin appliqués for which Arnakotak paid her money. In addition to making *kamiks* (boots), sealskin wall hangings and bags with cut-out ornamental details, beadwork became the most recent addition to her range of crafts. Alma tells about exceedingly beautiful slipper uppers with ornate beadwork that Kenojuak crafted.

Like other goods that came from the South, the little glass beads they used were not always available in sufficient quantity. In the winter of 1957-58, the women ran out of the materials they needed for their work. Alma (as she mentions herself) therefore encouraged Kenojuak to try her hand at drawing.

According to Alma, Kenojuak was hesitant at first, claiming that she could not draw and that drawing was a man's business anyhow. Nevertheless, she eventually accepted the office stationery that was offered to her. The next time Kenojuak visited the Houstons' home, where one of the rooms served as a sewing centre, she took the sheets of paper with her. They were filled with delightful, interlinking pencil sketches (the kind of compositions that can be seen in the prints of Kenojuak's drawings dating from 1960). Full of excitement, Alma went running into the print shop to show them to her husband.[24]

In Kenojuak and James Houston's recollections of events it was James Houston who appealed to Kenojuak one day, when she was handing in some more craft work, to at least give drawing a try. He gave her a few sheets of paper and drawing pencils in a plastic bag for her to take back to Kiattuuq. She hesitated because she had not the foggiest notion what she was supposed to draw. At that, Houston suggested that she simply sketch anything that came into her head. Kenojuak could not resist his urging. This was the time around Adamie's birth (in 1959), and when we ask Kenojuak if she was probably the first woman in Cape Dorset to begin drawing she replies (a little hesitantly) that she was indeed. The Houstons confirm the same fact in their writings.

The first pencil drawing that she put to paper in the camp, she tore up. However, she showed the following attempts to James Houston the next time she went to Cape Dorset. She felt greatly encouraged by the praise he lavished on these first efforts, and decided to continue.

In the catalogue *Cape Dorset Annual Graphics Collection '79*, Kenojuak adds, "I think I was one of the first ones to start drawing. I just drew anything. I think Saumik [James Houston] asked me to start making drawings because I used to make people and igloos and things like that out of sealskin [i.e., inset pictures and designs in different shades of sealskin]. I guess that's how he got the idea I could draw. The first time Saumik gave me a piece of paper and asked me to start drawing. I asked him what kind of a drawing am I going to make. And then he just told me to draw anything that comes into my mind – it could be anything. A lot of times I didn't know what to draw." Earlier, in the 1977 catalogue, she described her fear of the empty sheet of paper thus: "I was afraid to begin the first drawings because I had no idea in mind. It is often hard to draw and it is very hard to draw while you have to think." Kenojuak is not alone with such fears – Pitseolak Ashoona expresses herself in a similar vein: "Does it take much planning to draw? Ahalona! It takes much thinking, and I think it is hard to think. It is hard like housework." [25]

When Kenojuak started drawing, first successes could be foreseen in her attempts to make prints of Inuit sketches and drawings; however, a foremost concern was to find suitable motifs. Kenojuak's first print was based not on a design, but on a silhouette cutout that she had made as an appliqué for a sealskin bag. This was how she had done 'Rabbit Eating Seaweed' in 1958. In his *Confessions of an Igloo Dweller*,[26] Houston tells about how, one summer evening at Cape Dorset beach, an old boat of the kind used by trappers landed at low tide on the slippery rocks covered with long strands of seaweed. He observed how Kenojuak, with a child in her *amautiq*, got out of the boat and helped several other children out as well. As she walked over to the beach, Johnniebo anchored the boat.

Houston followed Kenojuak along the beach. Her behaviour betrayed none of the strains and sorrows of the years gone by; walking before him he could see a cheerful woman who had remained remarkably young. He caught up with her and they exchanged greetings. His attention was then attracted by the sealskin bag hanging over her shoulder. It was similar to the normal Inuit bags, yet there was something different about it. Houston asked if he could have a closer look at the bag. A dark picture carefully cut from scraped seal skin was sewn with sinew thread onto the bag, the latter made of seal leather, slightly dyed by tanning and turned inside out. Houston asked "What's that?" "A rabbit thinking about eating seaweed," replied the young woman.

By then, the printing project had made significant progress. In December 1958, the first set of prints from the years 1957 and 1958 were put on the market by the Hudson's Bay Company in Winnipeg. Unfortunately, no catalogue was made of the prints, and hardly any were documented. For sure, however, there were no prints by women in the collection.

Nineteen fifty-nine was the year in which a kind of competing enterprise was established as an alternative to the monopolistic control exerted by the Hudson's Bay Company. This new, efficiently run company belonged to the Inuit themselves and was organized as a co-operative in which anybody could participate. This 'West Baffin Eskimo Co-operative' held out the promise of achieving much better living conditions. The Inuit now had a supermarket they themselves operated. Even more important, however, was the artists' co-operative founded at the same time with help and advice from James Houston – Sanaunguabik, 'the place, where things are made.' It started business and soon the first sales were being generated with sculptures, drawings and prints. As payment for the work they supplied to the co-operative, the members received paper vouchers with which they could go shopping in the co-op supermarket. Another benefit produced by the extra competition was that the Hudson's Bay Company (now the 'Northern') rapidly cut its prices to a level similar to those of the former Baffin Trading Company.

That same year, the co-operative brought out a set of prints and published its own catalogue; this was the first 'Cape Dorset Annual Collection.' It was presented to a broad public audience in the spring of 1960, with an exhibition in the Montreal Museum of Fine Arts. When the Collection '59 was exhibited once again in Stratford, Ontario, and caused a sensation on the art market, the Inuit in Cape Dorset were encouraged along this path.

This time around, there were also two women represented by prints in the collection – Kenojuak and Kunu, her aunt-in-law. In those days, there were only two other women who worked on paper: Pitseolak Ashoona and her daughter Napatsi [Napachie]. Referring to those early days, Kenojuak tells us, "I usually only drew in daylight, sitting in our *qarmaq*. Though I was highly motivated, my role as mother and wife was even more important than this beautiful new work."

Kenojuak's prints are not made by the artist herself. Instead, they are prints made by stone cutters and printers on the basis of drawings by Kenojuak. Engravings or etchings, copperplate engravings, linocuts or woodcuts are the only work that the artist herself transfers to plate. But these, too, are not printed by herself personally; she has never been directly involved in the actual printing process.

The print of 'Rabbit Eating Seaweed' was made by first transferring the design on a larger scale from the sealskin bag to paper. This was probably done by James Houston himself. The next step involved one of the men in the print shop – most likely Osuitok Ipeelee – making a cardboard stencil from the paper copy. Finally, the actual printing work was performed by Iyola Kingwatsiak.

It is important to realize in this connection that the first drawings by Cape Dorset Inuit were often rather crude, and, at that time, nobody was thinking about making art prints anyway. However, Houston was obviously very impressed by the plain lines of Kenojuak's bag drawing, and he saw in precisely this work a specimen of typical graphic design. Perhaps it was this aspect that moved him to foster particularly template- or stencil-based work among the Inuit. In any case, making prints from drawings developed rapidly in the course of the late 1950s to become an important source of income for the Inuit.

It goes without saying that not every drawing is suitable for transfer. The issue is not so much the quality of the original – not every good drawing makes a good print. In James Houston's days, many drawings were produced without the artist giving any thought whatsoever to a potential transfer into print; even today, Inuit artists do not always consider this option when drawing. Moreover, the artists are usually not involved when it comes to selecting the drawings and titles for print making; this job is the responsibility of the co-operative managers.

In her first drawings, Kenojuak usually portrayed subjects that are well known from her sealskin appliqués and essentially bound to tradition –people, faces, *qarmaqs* and igloos, sled dogs and *qamutiks* (sleds), fish and birds. The West Baffin Eskimo Co-operative is still in the possession of some black-and-white photographs of two bags, likewise lost, that document this approach; one shows the silhouette of a human being with a hood, four-legged animals (dogs), birds from the side (geese) and the other mask-like faces, a fish, a whale, more dogs and birds, including stylistic elements that have characterized her work to this day. James Houston kept a drawing he made of the bag with the famous rabbit eating seaweed,[27] and in an early version of a film made about Kenojuak, one can see at Johnniebo's side another of her sealskin designs, preserved in this way for posterity.

Over the past forty years, Kenojuak has sketched birds in a never-ending variety of ways; owls, in particular, have always fascinated her. In addition, Kenojuak's bird drawings are particularly well suited for prints – a major reason for the sheer number and diversity of birds in her prints and her fame as a drawer of birds. Many admirers of modern Inuit art know Kenojuak almost purely as a bird drawer, but this does not do her justice. Although many annual collections contain samples of her work featuring birds, alongside them one can also find a large number of other subjects from Inuit culture – including pictures with no birds at all.[28] Kenojuak draws entire figures – or just faces and heads. Human beings, spirits, transformed beings, the sea goddess Talilayuk, animals (dogs, bears, wolves, foxes, hares, musk-oxen, walrus, whales, seals, fish and birds), as well as the sun and moon, *qarmaqs* and igloos, sleds, plants and leaves, harpoons and fishing rods, lamps, *ulus* and snow knives – she uses all these to depict forms, structures and compositions of unending novelty.

We find it remarkable in this connection that Kenojuak is known to many collectors by virtue of her prints only, even though she has created outstanding work in virtually every field of Inuit art (including dolls and the craft work she did in the 1950s). After all, her extremely rare stone sculptures, for example, which, like her drawings, she began to produce around 1959 after being urged by James Houston, now command high prices in the art trade.

In Kenojuak's more recent drawings, the number of different motifs has noticeably declined in comparison to her early work. Whereas she used to portray a growing number of objects in diverse combinations, in the course of time she has concentrated on the variants of the same subjects and perpetually new ways of seeing them – mainly human faces and animals, especially birds. This development, as we realize when talking to her, is mainly because Kenojuak professes her particular preferences and loves to an ever-greater degree, and also has the courage to stick with that.

Kenojuak sees the source of her inspiration in her experiences and memories, lending artistic expression to them through her powers of imagination. Scenes, objects and living beings of the Arctic are all familiar to her from her own experience, and some ideas and motifs are rooted in her fantasies and dreams. While spirits, transformed beings and shamanist images certainly stem from her ability to feel the deep-seated belief among the Inuit in the supernatural and in the powers of shamans, she admits to us that she knows no more about shamanism than anyone else.

Scenes based on traditional Inuit stories and legends, or on old Inuit myths, such as those often portrayed by other artists, are rarely featured in Kenojuak's drawings. Her explanation is that she heard this oral tradition from her grandmother but has forgotten it in the meantime. In May 1980, she even emphasized to Jean Blodgett that she does not weave old stories traditionally passed on into her work as a matter of principle, or at least not intentionally. She does not want to depict things that, owing to her own ignorance, fail to reflect the truth or that are inexact is some way.[29] The only legendary being in Kenojuak's work so far is therefore the sea-goddess Talilayuk ('Sedna' in English); after all, she saw the goddess with her own eyes, when as a child she glimpsed her head and flowing hair between the floes of ice.

Narrative elements, or even the retelling of things she herself has experienced, are absent on the whole in Kenojuak's work. Objects do not interact, but are merely part of a scene depicted in its entirety. One also looks in vain for self-portraits and drawings of her family. Even Talilayuk does not appear as a legend, but as part of a composition. 'They are happy to eat together,' her drawing for the Catholic mass book, shows Inuit people, men, women and children, eating seal meat together in an igloo; this is a scene, but not a narration – the people are grateful for the meal.

Anyone looking for a deeper meaning behind the objects that Kenojuak draws is approaching her graphic work with false assumptions. She draws a bird, a camp, a person, and combines parts to form a whole work of art. Often, therefore, different portions of the drawing will develop simultaneously. In the May 1980 interview with Jean Blodgett cited previously, she explains, "And rather what I do is I try to make things which satisfy my eye, which satisfy my sense of form and colour. It's more an interplay of form and colour which I enjoy performing and I do it until it satisfies my eye and then I am on to something else." [30]

In one report by James Houston, however, we find a brief, precise comment that "when she was asked how she would define art, Kenojuak, a young mother and now a famous artist, replied with breathtaking directness, 'The making of prints, what you call art, is simply to transfer the real to the unreal.' " [31]

As previously mentioned, Kenojuak's Uncle Niviaqsi was the first member of the immediate family to bring drawings and pictures to paper, shortly after the film called 'The Living Stone' was made with him in Cape Dorset by the National Film Board (NFB) in 1956. It was an exciting time because the Inuit sensed that something very new for them was in the making, something that could integrate their tradition and the modern age.

Niviaqsi died hunting in 1959. Although polar bear footprints were found around his body, there were no signs of mutilation or evidence of a fight. The cause of his death remained a mystery. Kunu, his wife, received news of death when she was down South being treated for tuberculosis.

In the warm summer days of the same year, Kenojuak gave birth to Adamie. Before her long, severe illness, she had borne three children (Jamasie, Mary and Qiqituk) but all of them had died. The boy, Kadlarjuk, too, was dead. This meant that Adamie was now her first living child since she had adopted Arnaguq. Her labour pains came on in Kiattuuq, but Peter Pitseolak was concerned, packed the mother-to-be into his boat and took her as fast as possible to the health centre in Cape Dorset.

They arrived late that evening, and by midnight the child was already born. It was Kenojuak's first delivery without the help of traditional midwives. Adamie has loved hunting ever since he was first allowed, at the tender age of three, to go with his father Johnniebo, but he has also inherited his parents' artistic gift.

Kenojuak's mother Silaqqi has been living with Iqalik, the daughter she bore in 1949, in Camp Kiattuuq for one year. There she, too, began to draw a little, but then she fell ill with tuberculosis and had to be taken to hospital in the South.

Johnniebo became more and more dissatisfied with daily life in the camp. Peter Pitseolak kept him busy as a kind of servant and gave him many tiresome duties to perform. Johnniebo's brother Towkie had already drawn the consequences from Pitseolak's domineering style of behaviour and had left the camp; Elisapee, his wife, had died of tuberculosis shortly before in the South (in 1959), and he was now living on his own in Camp Itilliaqjuk.

Itilliaqjuk:
The last years in camps

Johnniebo and Kenojuak thus had reason enough to turn their backs on Kiattuuq. In the year 1960, they, too, vacated their *qarmaq* and moved to Camp Itilliaqjuk. The leader there was Aoudla Pee, a personality very different to Peter Pitseolak. Johnniebo and Kenojuak swore never again to return to Kiattuuq to live.

Half a year after moving to Camp Itilliaqjuk, in the winter of 1960-61, Kenojuak gave birth to a baby girl called Aggeok; the child lived for only a few months and died in the Iqaluit hospital. In order to console Kenojuak, Johnniebo consented in 1962 to adopt a second boy, the son of Nee Itulu from Iqaluit. He was given the name Ashevak after Johnniebo's father. But this child, too, was granted only a short life. He fell ill after a few months. The fall's rough sea and inclement weather prevented him from being transported to the health centre in Cape Dorset, and so he died in the camp. The following year, 1963, Kenojuak gave birth to Elisapee Qiqituk; the babygirl died just the day after her birth.

Since the early 1960s, snowmobiles[32] had increasingly replaced the dog teams in Cape Dorset. Johnniebo also purchased one of these 'modern' vehicles. Kenojuak, on the other hand, could not get accustomed to these 'motorized land vehicles' (unlike motorboats) to such an extent that she herself would drive one. "To this day I have never driven a snowmobile or an ATV [nowadays a four-wheeled scooter in most cases[33]] myself; I have always been the passenger," she laughs, and goes on:

I have nothing against snowmobiles; after all, they're very useful. But what I can't approve of is that mothers with small children in their *amautiqs* drive such vehicles themselves. I consider that to be very dangerous.... At that time I just learned how to handle a rifle and shoot caribou. In those days, caribou came near our camp and into this area much more than now, but I had never seen one of them close up. One day, my brother Adamie Alariaq, his wife Nakasuk, my young son Adamie and I set out by snowmobile to hunt. When we discovered a caribou, my brother and his wife crept up on foot behind it and left me and the boy behind with the sled. But as things happen, the caribou made a turn and came running straight towards our sled. Adamie threw himself on the ground beside the sled because he was afraid of the animal storming up on us. But just then my brother shot it.

When all of us set to skinning the animal, three more caribou came closer to the place where we were. Adamie and Nakasuk began to shoot at them while I simply stood beside them and watched. Then my brother asked me with surprise, "Why don't you grab one of the rifles?" So I took one and started shooting as well. I remember feeling really proud and happy afterwards.

While they were staying in Camp Itilliaqjuk, James Houston talked to her about the National Film Board (NFB) expressing interest in making another film in Cape Dorset after 'The Living Stone.' It was intended that the film should deal not only with Inuit art, but in general with the traditional Inuit way of life; Johnniebo and Kenojuak had been chosen as leading actors.

The two consented gladly and in the spring of 1962 came to Cape Dorset, where accommodation was provided for them and the three children, Arnaguq, Adamie and Ashevak. Every day for three months they worked with the film team; the result was the film 'Eskimo Artist– Kenojuak.' [34]

Kenojuak usually carried a cushion in her *amautiq* instead of little Ashevak, whom she left to be cared for in the health centre during the day, but who would notice that in the film anyway? Once, the whole team travelled by dog sled to Camp Itilliaqjuk in order to film 'realistic' camp scenes. However, it was now late spring, so they had to make the igloo shown in the film out of polystyrene; the snow was already much too soft to build a snow house.

Kenojuak found the constant repetition of film scenes and having to wear the same clothes all the time to be rather tiring. However, Johnniebo was finally able to use the fee they had earned to buy a canoe owned by Lukta Qiatsuq. Johnniebo had been trying for many years to be independent of others; now he could hunt on its own . It was like a new beginning.

Nineteen sixty was the year that Terry Ryan, a graduate of the Ontario College of Art, began working in the Co-op Art Centre. The following spring, Alma Houston was the first to leave the Cape Dorset settlement with her children; they were supposed to attend a 'proper' school. Some time later, James Houston also accepted a new task at Steuben Glass in New York City and left Baffin Island. Terry and his first wife, Patricia, were excellent successors, and in 1962 Terry became the chief manager of the West Baffin Eskimo Co-operative. For the Inuit, the departure of the Houstons was an incisive and sad event. Friendships of many kinds had grown over the years, and in the course of the decade gone by, the Houstons had given important impetus that greatly affected life in the settlement, changing it for the better.

At the end of 1961, Qiatsuq tried to engrave drawings on copper plates for the first time and it was not long before Kenojuak also received this material for experimentation. She carved directly into the metal, and she had to use tools that were totally new to her. It was quite difficult at the beginning, but she gradually gained experience and practice in transferring her delicate pictures straight to the plate. Sometimes she would draw a pencil outline on the plate before engraving the permanent line.

Johnniebo, who had also done paper drawings before, now followed suit and began to grapple with copper engraving as well. The two of them would transport the copper plates to their home in Camp Itilliaqjuk, engrave them, then bring them back again to the print shop in Cape Dorset. "Engraving on copper was pretty tough on the muscles," confesses Kenojuak.

The winter of 1963 was extremely hard. The drifting ice made hunting extremely difficult and dangerous, and one could no longer rely on the fur trade. In order to avoid the worst economic distress, Johnniebo and Kenojuak shifted their energies more and more to drawing, or worked on sculptures if they had suitable stone as material.

Whenever they visited Cape Dorset to shop, something that always took a number of days, Arnaguq and Adamie would attend the school. The boys would then return to camp with homework and text books; they now learned things that were unfamiliar or indeed totally unknown to their parents – and that would remain so.

In early 1965, Johnniebo and Kenojuak adopted a little girl by the name of Pee from Ijitsiaq [Eegeetsiak] Peter and his wife, Nitani; Kenojuak had accompanied the mother to the health centre and waited there with her for the baby to be born. That was around the time when the Royal Canadian Mounted Police opened a police station in Cape Dorset and stationed a 'Mounty' there.

A few months later, when fall set in, Kenojuak was delivered in the health centre of her own daughter, Pudlo; Patricia Ryan assisted her as a nurse.

Johnniebo was quite spellbound by this healthy and robust child. In his friendly and open-hearted way, he often took both girls, almost the same age, in his strong arms and carried them around. He loved them tenderly. Soon the weather worsened, winter signalling its approach with frequent snowfalls. In the canvas tent, their lodging in Cape Dorset, it was now becoming more and more uncomfortable, and so not long after Pudlo's birth the whole family returned to Camp Itilliaqjuk.

Soon after their arrival, Tuqlik Akesuk, the aged father of Latchaolassie, was torn from their midst by influenza. He had gone almost completely blind in his last years, but still kept on carving stone until the very end – trusting only in the feel and touch of his hands.

Kenojuak was expecting yet another baby in 1966 when the nurses advised her urgently, on account of her poor state of health, to move to the Cape Dorset settlement. Since compulsory education for the two older boys was drawing closer and closer, there could only be one decision: the whole family gave up living in Camp Itilliaqjuk, to which they had become very attached. Kenojuak grieved deeply – for her the departure meant the end of an era and an entire way of life.

IV

In the settlement

Kinngait:
Living in solid houses

Radical changes had occurred in Nunavut, the land of the Inuit, within a very short time. Whereas the life led by Kenojuak's forefathers had been based entirely on the open land and the adjacent sea, her parents' generation by contrast was becoming more and more dependent, mainly as a result of fur trading and bartering on goods and equipment from the South. After the fur trade collapsed, the Inuit tried to revert once again to their traditional way of life, but they succeeded to only a marginal and inadequate extent. They were already influenced too much by these new experiences. It was true, of course, that the one or other Inuk had been able to sell sculptures prior to James Houston's arrival in Cape Dorset; yet the market was dominated and limited by the Hudson's Bay Company, the Baffin Trading Company and occasional buyers from the outside. It was only by the opening of the market initiated by Houston that the Inuit had, for the first time, a real and sustainable opportunity to gain financial security by dedicating themselves to art in times of distress, when hunting was to no avail. Kenojuak's life story is exemplary for this.

By the second half of the 1960s, almost all Inuit had left their traditional camps in the Sikusiilaq region, with the exception of short stays during the summer months; the last all-year camps were abandoned in 1971. People had then moved to the community of Cape Dorset, where they were offered housing by the so called Housing Program on particular terms (a kind of lease). The children could go to school regularly here, and health care was also available.

The life of the Inuit underwent total change. Rather than living in *qarmaqs*, igloos and tents, they now had heatable houses supplied with drinking water and electricity. If necessary, families received social security and for survival were no longer directly dependent on their hunting success; essential goods were available in the supermarkets. Whereas in the past, children learned the traditional way of life from their parents, now they spent most of their day in school or doing their homework.

Motorization became more and more prevalent. The Inuit used to travel across the land and the sea ice in sleds drawn by dog teams, and they now speed along in snowmobiles. Rowboats (*kayaks* and *umiaqs*) are replaced by motor-boats, and cross-country travel is done with ATVs. Caribou hunting is mostly confined to a single day now, whereas previously the men were away for a whole week. The dog teams, once vitally important for the existence of families, gradually disappeared; few people nowadays can afford the luxury of dogs because their food is so expensive (in the old days, they were mainly fed walrus meat, something that is rarely available now).

After temporary accommodation in a tent, Johnniebo, Kenojuak and their children moved into one of the typical houses of the early settlement period, referred to as 'matchboxes' on account of their small size and appearance. The house comprised three bedrooms only and had no additional rooms (it has since been demolished). Some time later, they moved into a larger house in the centre of the community that was more appropriate for the family. For Johnniebo, this was to be his last home.[35]

Johnniebo did not give up the traditional life completely when they moved to Cape Dorset, and continued to go out hunting and fishing to feed his family. Whenever she could, Kenojuak accompanied him out 'on the land.'

When their son Qiatsuq came into the world in December 1966, he was adopted by Aggeak Petaulassie and his second wife, Timangiak; Aggeak's first wife, Sheorak, the natural mother of Kenojuak's adopted son Arnaguq, had died in 1961 a mere 38 years old. Five months after the adoption, Timangiak herself gave birth, and this time their newborn son Jamasie was adopted by Johnniebo and Kenojuak. This was regarded as a 'fair swap' between the two families.

In the year 1967, Canada celebrated its centennial. At the recommendation of the Eskimo Arts Council, a portfolio of six engravings by Kenojuak was published to mark the occasion. The same year, at the age of 40, Kenojuak the artist was accorded special acclaim for the work she had produced to date. Terry Ryan and Jimmy Manning were the first to receive the message through their 'communication channel' that they then brought to Kenojuak, beaming with joy. On 24 November she was to be one of the first persons to be honoured with the new 'Order of Canada,' a medal of service honouring special achievements in all areas of Canadian life.

The journey to the South to receive the medal was the first since her stay in hospital more than ten years previously. She felt particularly secure now that Johnniebo accompanied her. On 8 November 1967 both of them flew to Ottawa, where they were warmly welcomed by Alma Houston. Before the ceremony, Kenojuak was understandably slightly nervous and timid, but when the award was finally presented to her she felt a sense of great pride.

In celebration of the conferral she and Johnniebo also attended the opening of an exhibition of her works at the National Library of Canada in Ottawa; 45 works by Kenojuak and 5 by Johnniebo were displayed.

Not long after, Kenojuak travelled to Ottawa once again, this time to have her eyes examined. She tells us about it with a bemused smile on her face.

> I was quite scared about it, although Johnniebo, my husband, was allowed to come with me into the doctor's consulting room. I was timid and restless and could not sit still on the examination chair. I think the doctor must have been wondering about me. But after an interpreter had told me how simple such an eye inspection is, I became quite calm all of a sudden. When I had to go to the eye specialist a second time, I was not frightened any more.

In May 1969, Johnniebo and Kenojuak and their three children Adamie, Pee and Pudlo flew to Ottawa yet again; soon they were rather familiar with the capital. The Canadian government had asked Kenojuak and Johnniebo to take part in the creation of a seven-meter by eight-meter stucco mural relief to adorn the Canadian pavilion at the 1970 Expo fair in Osaka. The whole family lived in an apartment. Every morning, a taxi would come and take the two little girls to a day nursery, Adamie to school, and the two artists to their work. They very much enjoyed having an Inuktitut interpreter at their disposal, and the air conditioning system in the rooms where they were working is something that Kenojuak still enthuses about.

The project took three months to complete, which gave them enough time on weekends to get to know the surroundings of Ottawa. Kenojuak met many old friends again, including Harold Pfeiffer and Sarah Ikummiaq. Fourteen years had passed since her hospital stay in Quebec and her homecoming aboard the *C. D. Howe*, on which Sarah had been travelling as an interpreter. Their conversations brought back many memories of those days. For Johnniebo and Kenojuak, the Expo '70 project had one very pleasing outcome – back in

Cape Dorset they were able to afford a new canoe equipped with an outboard motor.

Kenojuak gave birth to her last child, her daughter Silaqqi, in January 1970 at the hospital in Iqaluit (Frobisher Bay). However, she insisted on visiting Expo '70 in Osaka, to see the mural relief that she and Johnniebo had created for the Canadian pavilion.

In the same year, the Canadian Post Office issued a postage stamp bearing one of her drawings, 'The Enchanted Owl.' Two more stamps based on her drawings were to follow.

In 1970, after implementation of a project closely associated with the Inuit leader Abraham 'Abe' Okpik, a degrading phase in modern Inuit history in the Northwest Territories came to an end. From now on, the Inuit were no longer to be identified by numbers; finally, they were allowed to choose surnames for themselves. Many of the older folk took their former birth name as their surname, preceding it with a name from the Bible, and quite a number of household heads chose the name of their father as their new surname. In this same manner, Kenojuak became Kenojuak Ashevak (Johnniebo's father was called Ashevak), a name she bears with pride.[36]

Kenojuak paid two visits to Halifax in Nova Scotia, a city she particularly liked on account of its seaboard location. In October 1971, she and Johnniebo attended the opening of an exhibition of their respective works. Some time later, in February 1974, sculptures, drawings and prints by Johnniebo and Kenojuak were shown once again.

But this second time Kenojuak came alone. In the fall of 1972, Johnniebo had suddenly complained about strong stomach pains. He was brought to the health centre, where he lay two days and two nights. Thick, impenetrable fog made it impossible for a medivac plane to approach Cape Dorset. The third evening, 8 September 1972, Johnniebo died. An intestinal occlusion had developed, and only an operation could have saved him. On 23 September, Johnniebo was buried at the settlement's cemetery. Over his grave, marked by a cross bearing a syllabic inscription that reads 'Janivvu Asivaq | 1923 | 8.9.1972,' rises the mighty ridge of Kinngait. One's view to the north falls upon the Tellik Inlet, on Mallik Island and on the valleys and hills of Cape Dorset. Kenojuak will live for a while close by the cemetery, in a part of the community known as Kuugalaag, 'the Valley.'

After Johnniebo's death, Kenojuak herself is convinced that she would never have survived that first winter on her own. But friends and relatives stood by her and provided her and her children with food, especially that they brought with them from the hunt. After Johnniebo's death, she did not even want to go fishing again even though she used to enjoy it passionately. Her worried brothers and brothers-in-law were unable to tear her out of her lethargy. Then one spring, she was enticed by the birdsong she used to love listening to while fishing, and set out once again for the water. "It is so wonderful, to go fishing," she says.

Aggeok Pitseolak, her husband's sister, was particularly devoted to her during those hard days following Johnniebo's death, and she was also the one who finally encouraged Kenojuak in 1973 to move in with Etyguyakjuaq Pee. His wife had died giving birth some years before, and he also felt lonely. Now he would become a friendly and affectionate father for Johnniebo's children. However, their time together was to be short-lived. After several stays in a hospital down South, where he had to be treated for tuberculosis, Etyguyakjuaq died in Cape Dorset in 1977 during the summer solstice.

Around Christmas 1979, Kenojuak and her remaining six children moved in with Igiuk Joanassie – to her fourth house. The partnership with Igiuk was brief because he died only two years later of a brain haemorrhage, it is said. Arnaguq, who had already worked quite often in the Co-operative's print shop, had been making his own drawings for some considerable time. Adamie was active in observing weather conditions and occasionally carved stone sculptures. Pudlo and Pee, her adolescent daughters at that time, were not going to school any more, unlike the two youngest ones, Jamasie and Silaqqi. During the short summers, the family moved out to the old campsites to hunt and fish or, quite simply, to live as they used to 'in the old days.' Kenojuak's mother, Silaqqi, was still in relatively good health in those days, but blind in one eye like Quitsaq, her own mother. She was living with her son Quvianaqtuliaq, a half-brother of Kenojuak's, and his wife Nivi, a daughter of Johnniebo's brother Towkie.

Iqalurajuk:
Longing for the traditional life

When we came to Cape Dorset for the first time in early summer 1995, we had the great fortune to live as guests with Adamie and Ooloosie Ashevak. Both have a good command of the English language and made us acquainted with the land and its people. They took such pleasure in having us *qallunaat*, the first in their house, and in our knowledge about renowned Inuit artists about whom we were given further information at every opportunity. On this occasion, we also found out that Adamie was a son of Kenojuak Ashevak, whose work we greatly treasured even then.

His mother was not living in the settlement in those days. Instead, she was spending the days of spring 'on the land,' in a camp whose whereabouts we had not the slightest notion at that time (it was Iqalurajuk, as she herself later told us). Now, in the middle of June, the ice was no longer sufficiently firm to travel there by sled. At the same time, the sea was not yet open enough to enable one to go there by boat. So we were unable to meet Kenojuak personally. All we heard was her voice every day over the radio receiver.

One evening, when sitting together chatting about the 'old days,'[37] and life on the land, Ooloosie asked her husband to show us the NFB video of 'Eskimo Artist: Kenojuak.' And so, with this film dating back to 1962, Adamie introduced us to his parents, his brother, and himself as a two-year-old boy. We watched an artist family living on the land, travelling across the sea ice with the dog team and at the Co-op in Cape Dorset settlement. Deeply impressed, we noted in our diary:

The sounds of the wintry Arctic penetrate us deeply; pictures projected onto the tent walls by the play of shadows in the light of the *qulliq* fire awaken fairy tales from the bottom of our imagination; the close presence of people and dogs gives us with warmth and protection in the icy cold of the polar night. These are the impressions that caused Kenojuak to grow as an artist. We see how Terry Ryan, who joined the West Baffin Eskimo Co-operative in 1960 as an artistic advisor, fostered and supported her and her work. Her comments in the film reveal her world of thoughts – on the importance of hunting, for example: "He [a stone cutter] is happy to cut blocks for the Co-operative, but he is much happier to hunt. And the hunt is still the largest part of him." Or talking about sheets of paper for printing lithos, "A piece of paper from the outside world is as thin as the shell of a snow bird's egg." Or on the cosmology of the Inuit and the *qallunaat*: "Ay, look at that, we thought it [the moon] was flat, they think it's round. How strange to find the sun is so much farther away than the moon; we always thought it was the same distance. These people who made the sun's and moon's picture, they know the whole world and more. I know the world between here and our camp; that is all I know." We are all deeply moved by the film.

Our curiosity was awakened. In the days that followed, we found out more and more details about Kenojuak and the life of this 'artist in two worlds.'

The next year we did not meet Adamie and Ooloosie in Cape Dorset. Adamie was doing further training in the South, in Ottawa, so the whole family had moved to the Canadian capital. We were now living as house guests with Jimmy Manning, manager at the West Baffin Eskimo Co-operative, and his wife Pitseolala, a niece of Kenojuak's.

This time Kenojuak was in the settlement. Jimmy, who knew of our long-tended desire to get to know Kenojuak personally, arranged a first meeting for us. It was going on nine o'clock in the evening when, after a short walk, we arrived with Jimmy and Pitseolala in front of Kenojuak's house at the northern edge of the settlement – House No. 128 in the Itjurittuq part of the community. Kenojuak had relatives from Kimmirut staying with her, and so a large number of women friends from the settlement were there that evening to welcome the guests. When we entered the room, we first had to get our bearings in the smoke-filled air. Everyone was sitting smoking on the floor, playing bingo with faces hot with excitement. Only Kenojuak had taken a chair.

She came straight up to us and hugged us like trusted old friends; Adamie's friends were also her friends, she had Jimmy tell us. Before we could say anything, she explained to us, through our interpreter Jimmy, that Adamie had just called from Ottawa and had asked how we were getting on. She then asked one of her daughters to get him on the telephone for us. Only afterwards we were able to talk about what had led us to her – our wish to get to know her. However, so as not to keep her from her guests for too long, we just arranged a meeting for one of the evenings ahead; Jimmy would settle the details by phone.

When Jimmy called her in the morning of the day we had arranged to meet, we found out that Kenojuak had caught a cold and was running a temperature. It remained uncertain whether we could meet before our impending departure; in any case, Jimmy should call again towards ten in the evening. The next time Jimmy rang, Kenojuak was feeling significantly better. Since her guests were still there and she wanted to speak to us without disturbances, she would come to Jimmy's house. We arranged for her to be collected by car.

Kenojuak stayed for more than two hours, and Jimmy, in whom she obviously has absolute trust, helped us to overcome the language barriers. We explained to Kenojuak our plan to write a book about her life in two worlds, and after reflecting for a moment she responded with enthusiasm to our idea. That same evening we already decided together on a basic outline and some of the first details, and Kenojuak said she was looking forward to our next meeting.

In early spring of the year after, we arrive back in Cape Dorset, well-prepared, and find ideal conditions for our work. Kenojuak is expecting us, and Jimmy Manning has provided an experienced interpreter, his sister Jeannie. Kenojuak's nephew, Timmun Alariaq, and his wife Kristiina put their 'beach house' at our disposal, a very well furnished and cosy little house down at the beach, in which to stay and to conduct the many interviews. We find out, incidentally, that Johnniebo had helped erect this beach house back in 1950. It was originally built as the teacher's house, although considerably smaller at that time, and was first occupied by the Applewhites; so we are living and working on 'historical territory.'

It is also Timmun and Kristiina who take us on a three-hour, some eighty kilometer journey with snowmobile and *qamutik* to their Camp Iqalurajuk, the 'place of the few big fish' on the other side of Andrew Gordon Bay, and to long-abandoned camps where Kenojuak had once lived. By seeing things with our own eyes, we hope to sense a little of what the Inuit call 'the old way of life.' [38]
We spend days 'on the land,' with ten of us staying in Timmun's one-room but well-equipped cabin, enjoy 'native food' (caribou meat and Arctic char, raw and cooked), freshly baked bannock, go 'jigging' (ice-fishing) with our hosts,

and allow ourselves to be enthralled by the awe-inspiring, snow-covered landscape of the Arctic.

On one of these days, we travel by snowmobile across the ice to the southeast tip of Andrew Gordon Bay, past the towering palisades of ice and mountains of pressed ice formed along the coast by the tides, follow the directions of *inuksuit* (stone figures) high up on a mountain ridge, and finally manage to struggle through the chaos of fragmented ice to the shore. We have reached Camp Ikirasak, now abandoned, in which Kenojuak was born seventy years before, and which Pootoogook had made his home soon after for many years. The location was well chosen. Nestling between gently rising hills, on one of which an old sailing mast had been erected as a landmark, the camp lies on a ground that slopes gradually down to the sea, facing the sun, and slightly protected a little against the winds. All that remains of the camp, once filled with an abundance of life, are two crooked cabins made partly from material salvaged by Pootoogook from the *Nascopie*, the ship that went aground in 1947, and the timber frame of an old pentagonal *qarmaq*. The wind has driven snow through the windows and doors of the cabins; fresh tracks in the snow betray the recent visit of a polar bear in one of the cabins. In recent years, people from Cape Dorset have marked their names and dates indelibly on the walls. Timmun, smiling, pulls an old nail from the wall and scratches 'Polar Bear was here – April 1997' to add to the collection.

The artist comes to the Litho Shop nearly every day to draw

'Comparing Braids,' stonecut (1993)

'Birds Braid Woman's Hair,' lithograph (1994)

'Akkunnigani Timmiat [In Amongst The Birds],' lithograph (1995)

'Qimmuija [Like a Dog],' stonecut (1996)

'Shore Bird's Descent,' stonecut (1996)

'Small Tundra Bird,' stonecut (1996)

'Iqqaluiit [School of Fish],' lithograph (1996)

'Uppiit [Owls],' lithograph (1996)

'Arctic Assembly,' lithograph (1996)

'Tidal Spirit,' etching and aquatint (1996)

'Issharulik [Head with Wings],' stonecut (1996), with slate printing plate

'Issharulik [Head with Wings],' stonecut (1996)

'The Enchanted Owl,' the first stamp 1970 (from a stonecut made in 1960)

'The Owl,' the third stamp 1993 (from a drawing made in 1969)

'Falcon,' Serpentine (1997)

Depending on weather and ice conditions, the journey across Andrew Gordon Bay to Cape Dorset could be accomplished by snowmobile within three to five hours; however, traditional travelling by dog team as in Kenojuaks's childhood took two or three days, sleeping overnight in the 'travel igloo' that had to be erected in the evening.

On the return trip to Cape Dorset, we, too, cross Andrew Gordon Bay, working our way through the bizarre formations of broken-up pressed ice between Alareak Island and the southwest corner of the bay; the first thing we see is a rusty iron cube. We remain motionless before a cross standing on a mountain slope close to our route. The cross marks the grave of Jaku, who died in 1923. The general view was that a good man had passed away, one who had always helped others with food. Heavy frost made it impossible to bury him properly, so his body was placed in an old oil barrel that a whaling ship had left behind near the camp. He would have to lay in rest here for almost sixty years before his mummified corpse was finally buried in 1982.

The story of Jaku[39] extends far back to the time when the Inuit converted to the Christian faith, in which they tended to exaggerate many beliefs. Around the turn of the century, the leader at Camp Itilliaqjuq was a man named Simigak, who claimed to have met Jesus, having observed him hunting for seal one day. His people responded by building an enormous igloo, open to the sky, to assemble in for services. Simigak's cousin, Mamirajak, believed firmly in this second coming of the Lord and preached that Jesus had come as a messenger from God to look after his people. He himself was then dubbed Kigak, 'the messenger,' with the result that he simply felt even more confirmed. Kigak bean to sing in this enormous igloo, dancing around completely naked. He was obviously falling more and more into a state of ecstasy because he ended up announcing, "I am going up to heaven! Halleluja!" Simigak joined him, but made it very clear that "Not just you, but all of us are going up to heaven!"

Nobody went up to heaven, of course, but Kigak went on singing that everywhere, on this side and that side of the Hudson Strait, people were going up to heaven. For this reason, the people regarded him as an *angakkuq*, a shaman, since he was able to see what was happening in other places.

The men shaved off their beards and the women their hair, so as not to get caught on anything on the way up to heaven. Kigak's wife rubbed seal oil into her clothes in order not to be too clean, and everybody did the same – after all, had Okhamuk, the Reverend Peck, not preached that they should not hang on to possessions? Indeed, the people were acting drunk and started doing stupid things. Kigak, for example, is said to have jumped on a sleeping man's tummy, and would probably have trampled him to death if the man's son had not restrained him. The man himself had offered no resistance since Jesus on the cross had not offered any resistance either.

At some stage the people awoke from their trance. Kigak realized that his name as 'the messenger' was false and inappropriate, taking back his original Inuit name of Mamirajak and later his Christian name, Jaku.

Timmun, experienced in such excursions, steers our three unoccupied sleds through jagged barriers of rough ice that make it difficult to cross Kisabik, the old anchorage for whaling ships. We follow him on foot. After a short journey onwards we reach what used to be Camp Itilliaqjuq, whose leader in the early 1960s had been Aoudla Pee. This was the place to which Johnniebo and Kenojuak had turned in 1960 when they wanted to get away from Camp Kiattuq and Peter Pitseolak's domineering rule. All that can be seen of Aoudla's own camp, situated at the foot of a hill with an *inuksuk* on top, are the remnants of two *qarmaqs*; owing to the rough ice barriers at the shore, we are unable to proceed to the place where Johnniebo and Kenojuak had lived.

In the end, we approach Camp Saatturittuq. Here, Kenojuak had given birth to her second child, Mary, in 1949. Some time ago, Qaqaq Ashoona and his wife Mayoreak withdrew permanently to this camp, and it was here that Qaqaq died of heart failure in fall 1996. Passing Peter Pitseolak's former Camp Kiattuq, we reach the Cape Dorset settlement as darkness falls.

Many evenings we sit with Kenojuak and Jeannie in Timmun's well-heated beach house and speak about the past seventy years. Kenojuak is always exactly on time for the meetings we arrange with her; one could set the clock by her. We drink coffee or tea and empty one box of biscuits after the other, interrupt our discussions for a cigarette break outside the front door in the evening cold before returning to the cosy warmth of the oil-heated stove. Kenojuak and Jeannie clearly enjoy our gatherings and the atmosphere during our conversations. When the evenings come to an end, we call for the taxi; it is the only one in the community – a collection taxi with a platform behind, on which the younger passengers have usually taken their places. Kenojuak squeezes into the passenger compartment and waves to us through the dirty windows with her impish smile.

Who is Kenojuak? If one meets her in the street, there is nothing conspicuous about her, and she actually looks no different from the other women in the community. Nor is there any indication that an internationally recognized artist, honoured by many awards, is passing by. Yet when you come into direct contact with her, something significant changes – you are charmed by her self-confident cordiality and her humour. An indescribable gleam radiates from her eyes, signalling that she has recognized you. In this moment, if not before, you are captivated by the extraordinary personality of this woman. She must have had this impact on others already when James Houston encountered the young Kenojuak on the beach forty years ago and was so deeply impressed that he still makes reference to it in his writings. We, too, have been unable to escape her charisma since we first shook hands with her.

At closer quarters, however, we are made aware of how one-sided these first impressions can be; quite different facets of her personality then become apparent. When she suddenly unleashes her whole temperament, during a conversation, for example, she reveals layers of her soul that give us only an intimation of the eruptive forces that lull constrained and hidden from view in her deeper self. We then recall the stories about her father Usuaqjuk, the descriptions of his charismatic personality and his kind generosity, but also the forces that kindled in his soul and his occasionally demonic temperament.

Kenojuak tells us stories from her life, a life in two worlds – the traditional world of the Inuit and the modern world of the *qallunaat*. We talk in detail about recent years and the thoughts she has today. Due to the growing importance of her artistic work, she went on many travels after Johnniebo's far too early death. Prior to our conversations with her, friends in Cape Dorset had already prepared us for the fact that Kenojuak was an artist who also had a wealth of experience in dealing with *qallunaat*, internationally as well, and that she therefore knew the *qallunaat* world better than one might usually expect; nevertheless, we are astonished at the number of cities in Canada, the United States, Europe and Asia she had seen over the past three decades.

There was the meeting with Jessie Oonark, the well-known artist from Baker Lake, in Ottawa in the year 1976: drawings by the two artists had found their way into the Roman Catholic Sunday Missal, and the two women were then invited as guests at the Canadian Conference of Catholic Bishops. She also tells us how, in October 1977, she travelled with Kananginak Pootoogook to Toronto: The World Wildlife Fund (WWF) had commissioned the two of them each to contribute one of six prints to a portfolio that was then published as a limited edition. Kenojuak was also impressed by a transatlantic flight to Rotterdam in the Netherlands, where she attended the opening of the exhibition entitled 'The Inuit Print' in March 1980.

We ask about the most important events of the last few years.

> Worst of all was the loss of my grandson Uqittuq three years ago. He was a son of Pudlo's, and I had held him very dearly in my heart. His father Salomonie went out one beautiful day in April [in 1994] with his twenty-year-old girlfriend and the little boy on the snowmobile over to Mallikjuak for hunting. There was a sudden change in the weather and they couldn't see anything any more. They then broke all the rules and abandoned the snow-mobile – Salomonie wanted to go on foot and look for a way out. He was found in the end – frozen to death. The girl wrapped the boy in her parka, but it was no use. When the two of them were eventually found, the boy had already died of hypothermia. The girl survived. It was really terrible for me. Salomonie hadn't told me of his intention, otherwise I would have probably forbidden him to do so. I grieved deeply for a long time and couldn't say the child's name without crying. Only prayers helped me and friends around me who gave me comfort; my son Adamie, especially, was kind to me and brought me food.

When we ask, "Did this tragedy influence you, or even change your life?" she replies, "Before that, I hardly gave a thought to how other people cope when fate strikes. It is different now since the loss of my grandson Uqittuq. Now I try to support other people in sad situations the same way I was fortunate to experience." To the next question, "Has this tragedy also found expression in your art and even changed it?" Kenojuak answers, "I was physically affected; my soul suffered, too. But it found no expression in my art. I personally enjoy my artistic work – and the money I earn with which I can make my grandchildren happy. And I would like other people to enjoy my works and that they like them. But I don't express the experiences of daily life, or feelings and emotions in my drawings."

We go on to ask, "The loss of your grandson was tragic and a great burden. But is there an outstanding event that you have particularly happy memories of?" Kenojuak answers, "Hhhmmm, that was when I visited my son Adamie and his family, as well as some old friends, in Ottawa with my four-year-old granddaughter at Christmas 1996. I met Pat Ryan again, for example, and Sarah Ikummiaq; she was the Inuktitut interpreter on the *C. D. Howe* when I was returning from hospital in Quebec. The journey turned into a wonderful experience for me: I paid the air fare myself and for the first time we flew all on our own and without any accompaniment to the South. I proved this way that I am not dependent on others." She adds, "Adamie picked me up at the airport. When my granddaughter saw the first high trees there in the South, she was amazed at the 'huge plants,' but Adamie put her in the picture. 'These are trees!' It was simply great to experience something like that myself." – "Are you happy that Adamie and his family have now returned to Cape Dorset?" – "Hhhmmm, I did miss Adamie very much!"

Later on, back in Ottawa, we were told that during her Christmas visit Kenojuak had made it clear to her son that she could not do without him in Cape Dorset. Even if there were signs of a good career in Ottawa for himself and his family, his future lay in Cape Dorset. And that is how things turned out. A year later, Adamie did come back.

We change the subject to our stay in Adamie's house two years previously. At that time Kenojuak was 'on the land,' and now we learn that she was in Timmun's Camp Iqalurajuk and spent a wonderful time fishing Arctic char. "Once I was lying on the metre thick ice of the nearby lake and speared a huge char the length of my arm through an ice hole. But how was I supposed to pull up the fish, which was crosswise to the hole? In the end I let down a fish hook on a string and that way managed to hoist the fish lengthways through the hole to the surface. It was a lot of work, but well worth it!"

"And you also drew there? And carved stone?" – "I work in Cape Dorset. Ever since I've had the grandchildren in the house, and before that as well, I have usually gone to the Litho Shop to draw; I am undisturbed there. Occasionally, when the desire overcomes me, I also carve stone sculptures. When the weather is bad, I have a small canvas tent at the side of my house in Cape Dorset that serves as my 'studio;' otherwise I like to work on stone in the open air." She continues, "I always liked doing stone carvings, ever since Saumik [James Houston] encouraged me to do so – that was about 1959. Usually they are middle-sized sculptures. Eight years ago [approximately 1989], however, I had to have an operation on my hands; I got terribly frightened that I would never be able to draw again. Afterwards, in fact, my hands were not really suited to carving any longer, but fortunately I could still draw. Last fall, though, I started carving again and made two large sculptures. The stone was very heavy. My sons Jamasie and Arnaguq turned it back and forth for me, and in the end it got lighter anyway." Visualizing this situation we all have to laugh. Kenojuak explains to us how she prefers to use the traditional tools for carving, namely an axe, chisel and a file, although they do require a lot of strength. "But I find the modern electrical devices too dangerous." The next day, when we ask Jimmy Manning about these sculptures, he has to admit, unfortunately, that no photographs were taken of these most recent carvings before they were sent to a gallery in the South. So we do not get a chance to see them. On our next journey, however, we are lucky to acquire a very new carving, a falcon.

When continuing with questions we learn: "I consider working with seal skin or also carving to be easier than drawing – the line with a felt-tip pen or crayon is always final and unchangeable. With the other materials you can usually 'iron out' mistakes quite well; drawings are always fixed straight away, even when you are only using a pencil and an eraser."

When she is in the settlement, Kenojuak appears in the Litho Shop almost every day and draws, despite being more than seventy years of age. Black felt-tip pens, coloured pencils and occasionally a pencil are her preferred media. She used to work with water colours as well, occasionally, but they are not really her favourite; she finds the results too diffuse. Now and then engravings are emerging from her hands.

In the Litho Shop, she often meets other women artist friends, for example Mary Pudlat and Sheojuk Etidlooie, who sit here and draw just like herself. Sometimes they get to chat with Osuitok Ipeelee and other stone carvers when they deliver their latest sculptures.

Our next question: "Did Johnniebo influence your work? Weren't you usually together when you were making stone carvings and drawings?" Kenojuak: "No, we each worked for ourselves, quite individually. Each of us was doing something entirely independent. Moreover, Johnniebo's stone sculptures never really appealed to me. Or to be more precise, I didn't like all of my husband's works, and I never liked his carvings." Question: "What did Johnniebo think about your work?" Answer: " I do not know; he never commented on them. Actually, we never looked at what the other one was doing."

"But you did work together on the mural relief for the Canadian pavilion at Expo '70 in Ottawa?" – "Yes, that's true; we really did work together on that. But there were moments when I thought, 'Why does he work so slowly?' and I helped him then because I was getting really impatient." She laughs. "Maybe Adamie [her son] has inherited a bit of that. You have to put a bit of pressure on him, too, now and again," although she is quick to extenuate this comment by saying, "But I need breaks, too...."

Kenojuak has a wide diversity of obligations and interests, tasks for which she feels responsible. She loves life in the camp, free of all ties, and whenever she gets a chance to drive out onto the land, she takes it. This does not diminish in the slightest her pleasure in artistic creation, in drawing and carving objects in serpentine.

However, Kenojuak's life continues to revolve around her family, first and foremost. She is a mother and a grandmother, and in fulfilling these responsibilities she is proud to contribute to the family's upkeep. After all, arts and crafts are one of the only means to earn money in the North. Although art still is only one part of her life, it is a very important one; it gives her independence and enables her to provide security for her children and grandchildren not only today but also in the future. Kenojuak is well aware of the value of money. This is why she is grateful to all those people who are interested in her work, who admire it – and buy it. "I am convinced that art lovers will speak of my works when I am dead and gone," she tells us.

Kenojuak has received recognition primarily on the art market in the South, not among the Inuit in her immediate surroundings. Early and rapid acclaim for her work actually made her life in the community more complicated, to a certain extent. Here was a woman, and a young one at that, who was gaining remarkable fame. She came into money, even overtaking the elders and quite a few of the men who, in addition to hunting, were devoted like herself to art.

When we ask how many drawings she must have produced in the course of time, she reflects for a long time before answering, "I don't know. Many hundred, probably more than a thousand. I cannot say." From the documentary material at the West Baffin Eskimo Co-operative, especially its annual catalogues, it is possible to calculate to some degree of precision the number of etchings, stone cuts and lithographs made from her drawings. In the 39 years that have passed since 1959, Kenojuak has had about 225 prints in the much-coveted annual collections of the Co-operative. Numerous exhibitions have been held in North America, Europe and Israel. Since her works are sought after by museums and attract broad interest among collectors, the usual editions of 50 prints are generally sold out very quickly and can only be acquired for a high price tag at auctions. While the prices in the '96 Collection set by the Co-op for Kenojuak prints were around $600 (Canadian), the 'Enchanted Owl' of 1960, which became famous through the postage stamp, is fetching prices of between $10,000 and $15,000 after only 20 years; recently, in fact, as much as $35,000 are said to have been paid. In the World Wide Web on the Internet, some 300 entries can be accessed if one searches on the word 'Kenojuak.' [40]

Her international renown has hardly changed Kenojuak's way of life. Despite being recognized as one of the leading Inuit artists in Canada, she admitted to Jean Blodgett in May 1980,

> I do not really consider myself a drawer, or an artist, or a sculptress, or whatever. I wouldn't say that of myself except in conjunction with the other things that I do. I would say, well yes, I draw and I sculpt, and I do appliqué, embroidery, and needlepoint … Tomorrow, however, I put all that aside to go out jigging; I want to do that because I have fond memories of having done that in the past… I don't put any aspects of my experience first as the main thing. Being able to do embroidery and being able to go out on the land and all those other things are not secondary to being an artist." [41]

It may seem strange to hear an artist speak in these terms, but they mirror the traditional attitude among the Inuit. These people were only able to survive because they mastered many skills at the same time, from making their own weapons and clothing, building *qarmaqs* and igloos, hunting, fishing and trapping, as well as adding ornamentation to everyday objects. Artistic work always served a particular function in the profanity of everyday life or on the higher religious plane; *'l'art pour l'art'* would have been a luxury that could prove lethal in the hard living conditions of the Arctic. As far as we can observe, Kenojuak's attitude is by no means unusual. Inuit people of her own generation and to some extent of the subsequent generation continue to maintain their traditional flexibility, which may explain why they do not attach any real priority to artistic skills, even when these make an essential contribution to their livelihood.

Kenojuak emphasizes very clearly to us that she has her own artistic style, which others keep trying to imitate; she herself would never copy others. There are some artists she likes, whose work she got to know in the early 1950s in Dr. Pfeiffer's home in Quebec, or in 1967 at the National Gallery of Canada – Henry Moore, for example. Of the Inuit artists, she values Kananginak Pootoogook and Peter Pitseolak, among others, but does not draw on them for inspiration. She has a powerful imagination of her own. Moreover, Kenojuak is well aware of her artistic creativity and especially her originality. She has what we would call her own distinctive style.

We ask Kenojuak about her wishes regarding organizational matters, such as exhibitions of her work. "I don't know what I should wish for. I cannot complain, the exhibitions of my pictures run well, everything is well arranged without me being burdened by any costs. Even my hotel accommodation is paid for, and the meals that I eat. No, I cannot wish for things to be any better." One thing that has struck her is that the art galleries have recently intensified their security precautions and have even started to employ guards. Yet these changes did not disappoint her in any sense. She has seen the like at airports as well, and accepted this with the typical equanimity that the Inuit possess.

This prompts us to ask how she imagines things will develop. "The circumstances in which people live are changing wherever one looks. How do you assess the future in Nunavut, the land of the Inuit?" Kenojuak replies, "I fear that our land is facing very difficult times ahead. They may even be dangerous times for those who firmly believe in God because they will be plagued with doubts about what is right. I think people will be less happy in the future; only God can give people joy. I am reminded of the advice that Kiatainnaq gave me, a lay Anglican priest who died around 1980. He said, 'Even when new religious communities arise in people's distress, you must not be led astray from your

Anglican church. Some people will have insane religious ideas, but God has taught us not to condemn them.' "

Question: "From whom and from what do you expect difficulties to come?" Kenojuak: "I believe that the traditional Inuit way of life will be completely lost because even today there are only few people with a full command of the old way of life. People will suffer because they will not know how to hunt when they are hungry. And they will be hungry because prices for food and everything else are shooting up; inflation is rising more and more. In order to satisfy everyday needs you need a job, and to get a good job you need to have certain education. But we have a lot of people here who don't have any training at all; or all they have is incomplete school education or professional training." After reflecting a moment, she goes on, "It's not so easy keeping the kids in school. One of my nieces has been working for a long time at the Co-op. She doesn't have enough school education, but she works well and does everything the jobs requires – even when she finds it difficult to learn new things. Of course, there are people who learn by doing their job. But many have no job where they can learn something that enables them to take on other jobs. Unemployment will increase as a result. That, in turn, will be hard on people who are dependent on just a little social welfare, not even enough for a week, never mind a whole month." Another pause, then she says, "Not everyone can be an artist, after all. The cost of living is going up and up, so a lot of artists will find it difficult to buy the material they need for their artistic work."

She moves onto a different issue, saying, "Another problem in the community is the abuse of alcohol and drugs. The reason for that is that many young people are more interested in alcohol and also drugs than they are in religion. They need money, of course, in order to obtain alcohol and drugs." At which we ask, "This problem is very widespread, unfortunately, but we would not have expected it in Cape Dorset. How do drugs get here?" Kenojuak: 'I don't know how the drugs get here, but it is difficult to control and to stop it. No, I don't ask where the drugs come from, you simply hear about it. I don't need such things to live." We ask, "And what is your attitude to alcohol?", to which she replies, "Whenever I'm invited to dinner I like to drink a glass of wine with the others. I also used to have alcoholic drinks in the house, but then some people would come uninvited just to drink. So I did away with it; I also saw a risk of people breaking in merely because of the alcohol."

When, in conclusion, we express our hope that the establishment of Nunavut as a self-administrated Inuit territory will provide a boost for self-reliance and self-confidence in the future, she emphasizes once again, "A lot of people surely will find a way to shape their lives in a way that gives them satisfaction, but I am certain that the main problem will be financial in nature because the people will not earn enough to compensate for inflation." Jeannie begins to laugh and says, referring to the fact that Kenojuak had to buy herself a new washing machine only the day before, "I think that if you look into the future you won't be able to afford any new washing machine or new dryer." To which we reply, "Next time we are going to inspect the washer," since Kenojuak has invited us to her house.

The first snow buntings are already back, twittering their song from the telephone wires, when one Saturday afternoon we are guests in Kenojuak's home. She has been living in this house in the Itjurittuq area, her fourth in Cape Dorset, since 1979. She moved here with six children, of whom only Jamasie and Silaqqi are still living as singles with their mother. This is compensated by the many grandchildren who liven up the place. Kenojuak's daughter Pudlo had three children from her marriage; her son Uqittuq, born in 1988, was killed three years ago, but her two girls, born in 1989 and 1992, live with their grandmother. Kenojuak's young grandson, Towkie, a bright boy and the adopted son of Adamie and Ooloosie, whom we got to know in his parents' house in 1995, frequently stays here as well. During our visit, too, he was romping about the house with his cousins.

Pudlo herself lives in Salluit with her boyfriend. Arnaguq and Adamie each have their own household in Cape Dorset. Pee is married and is now called Pee Mark; she has found a new home in Ivujivik, northern Quebec, with four of her children; two other children were given to relatives for adoption.

Kenojuak tells us with obvious enjoyment about the many honours that were being conferred on her over the last twenty years again and again, and at our request she puts on her various decorations so as to proudly show them to us, but mainly for a photograph in our book. At the same time we hear that her first major decoration, the Order of Canada, was stolen from her house years ago when she was away on the land. In those days, people did not normally lock their homes. It may have been children who got into the house; in any case, no trace of the thieves was ever found. Meanwhile the house has been secured with strong locks.

In 1974 she was elected to the Royal Canadian Academy of Arts, and in 1982 was nominated for the 'Companion to the Order of Canada.' In 1990, she was commissioned by the Department of Indian Affairs and Northern Development to create a lithograph, in a limited edition of three, entitled 'Nunavut Qajanartuk' (our beautiful land) – to commemorate the signing of the Inuit land claim treaty between the Tungavik Federation of Nunavut and the Government of Canada that same year.

Outstanding events include the conferral of an Honorary Doctorate by The Queens University in 1991, during the ceremony of which she was proud to wear the black cap and gown, and the Honorary Doctorate of Law conferred by the University of Toronto 1992. "Here I wore a red gown with white braidings. Both times I felt extremely honoured and proud. I did not feel the same nervousness any more at these ceremonies as I did when I first received the Order of Canada," Kenojuak tells us with a laugh.

In the same year, 1992, she was entrusted with creating the litho called 'Nunavut' (Our Country), once again limited to 3 copies, for the ceremonial signing in 1993 of the Tungavik Federation of Nunavut Settlement Agreement in Iqaluit.

With eyebrows raised high and eyes shining, she tells us about how she received the 'National Aboriginal Achievement Award' in Vancouver in 1995 for her 'lifetime achievement.' At the ceremony, she received a gold medal on a red ribbon, and an inscribed stele. "This award makes me especially proud."

She was accompanied on the journey to Vancouver by Jimmy Manning. Since he had recently told us a funny anecdote about a flight with Kenojuak, we surmise that this may have happened on the journey to Vancouver. But Kenojuak puts us straight: "No, no, that was much earlier – in 1990." She goes on to tell us the story the way she experienced it: "Jimmy and I were returning from the United States. We had arrived in Toronto and were boarding a plane that was to take us to Ottawa. I was relying totally on Jimmy because he is a much more experienced traveller than I. He can speak English to the people and make himself understood whereas I can't. In short, we got into the plane but saw nobody else besides ourselves getting in. Yet it was a gigantic jet with many seats. When we were inside and looked around, we were the only people on board.

Something had to be wrong – more than one hundred seats and only we two passengers. Perhaps the plane wasn't flying at all? Just then, a stewardess came up to us and Jimmy asked whether we were in the right place. She simply said, 'Yes!' Everybody had already taken the previous flight and so we flew to Ottawa with the plane to ourselves."

On the way home, we were still laughing away at the thought of how Kenojuak and Jimmy must have felt on that flight.

A few days later, our stay in Cape Dorset comes to an end. The evening before our flight, Jimmy Manning announced he would come by 'after dinner' to our beach house. We appreciate this gesture very much and are happy because for the Inuit this is how one honours the host. In our culture, it is the other way round – people are honoured by being invited. Jimmy comes not only with his wife Pitseolala and his little son, but also, quite unexpectedly and therefore all the more joyfully welcomed, with Kenojuak. They insist on an official farewell to their friends. Pitseolala had baked apple and cherry pie early that morning, before going on duty in the health centre, and brought it with her as an evening dessert.

Jimmy wants to know, quite understandably, how we are getting on with our work. We show him our tapes and notes, and I say with a laugh, 'You see, the only thing I'm missing is a conclusion – maybe one by Kenojuak." To which he replied, "Well, how about quoting her foreword to our 1993 catalogue?"

Here is the quote: [42]

The light is still on in the printmaking shops in Cape Dorset. Remember, I was one of the very first people to start drawing – only with pencils. Oh, it was so hard getting coloured pencils in those wonderful years. I remember when I first saw coloured crayons. I think one of the girls got them from the school. They brought a good, unusual smell to our small "Qamak." Before I even thought of drawing, I used to like the little flowers that grow during the very short summers we have.

I will never forget when a bearded man called Saumik approached me to draw on a piece of paper. My heart started to pound like a heavy rock. I took the papers to my Qamak and started marking on the paper with assistance from my love, Johnniebo. When I first started to make a few lines he smiled at me and said "Inumn," which means "I love you." I just knew inside his heart that he almost cried knowing that I was trying my best to say something on a piece of paper that would bring food to the family. I guess I was thinking of the animals and beautiful flowers that covered our beautiful, untouched land.

I have been working on paper, and sometimes carving for thirty long years. Those days seem a long way away now. It seems like I am running out of thoughts. Our community life has changed so much. When I bring drawings to the Co-op, I often say I'm running out of ideas, but Jimmy [Jimmy Manning] keeps telling me not to run out yet, and that there are still thoughts and good ideas that I have not yet come up with.

Pudlo (Pudlat) died this year. He always had different ideas, and drew images that relate to the changing life around him. Mayoreak (Ashoona) still draws of the old way of life. She and Soroseelutu (Ashoona) live a more traditional life out in the camp all year 'round. Now Simeonie (Kopapik) is the oldest person in the community [he also died in 1993]. He has three prints in the collection. When I look around at who is still drawing, it feels like we are babysitting, waiting for the departed ones to come back. Knowing that they are not coming back, it feels like the light is getting smaller and smaller.

Kavavaow (Mannomee) is one of the younger artists who works hard. I would very much like to tell the younger children growing up that they too have to try hard to work on paper. I think it's much easier now, because materials are here and you can go for training.

We are happy once again to be able to come up with a collection. We have worked hard with the printmakers, and we have to thank everyone who works on the prints.

That's all I have to say. Nakoumik, merci, thank-you.

Annex

Notes on the chapters

[1] Pitsoleak, Peter & Eber, Dorothy H., *People from Our Side*, p. 49.

[2] ibid., p. 118 ff..

[3] ibid., p. 118 ff..

[4] ibid., p. 119 ff..

[5] ibid., p. 92 ff..

[6] Aggeok's maternal grandmother (Annie Qimmaluq).

[7] Aggeok's paternal grandmother (Kaniak).

[8] Pitseolak, Peter & Eber, Dorothy H., *People from Our Side*, p. 27 ff..

[9] ibid., p. 75.

[10] Zoologically speaking, there are only two fox species on Baffin Island – the red fox (Vulpes vulpes) and the Arctic fox (Alopex lagopus). However, the red fox is present in three variants: red, cross and silver or black fox, and the Arctic fox is the only member of the Canidae family whose fur changes colour from brown to white as summer changes to winter. During the winter phase of the Arctic fox, about one percent of the population forms an additional blue variant (coloured grey to black-blue).

[11] Details about Qimuakjuk's fate are written down in Dorothy H. Eber *When the Whalers were Up North*. There is nothing to be found in available sources about Alainga's subsequent life.

[12] Bannock is a tasty kind of white bread, flat as pancake in shape and unacidified. It is made by heating a frying pan until it is very hot and then melting copious amounts of lard in it. The dough, consisting of flour, fat, a little water and raising agent, is then placed in the pan and fried golden-brown on both sides, adding more lard.

[13] Pitseolak, Peter & Eber, Dorothy H., *People from Our Side*, p. 133 ff..

[14] ibid., p. 139

[15] ibid., p. 141.

[16] Norman J. Macpherson, *Dreams and Visions*, p. 71 ff..

[17] James Houston has described the trek in his *Confessions of an Igloo Dweller*.

[18] Kenojuak remembers the names Mialia, Isaaci and Natsiapik.

[19] Houston, *Confessions of an Igloo Dweller*, p. 263 ff..

[20] ibid., p. 263

[21] ibid., p. 264

[22] ibid., p. 265

[23] ibid., p. 265

[24] See Blodgett, *Kenojuak*, p.32.

[25] Eber (Ed.), *Pitseolak: Pictures out of my life.*

[26] loc. cit. 226 ff..

[27] See Houston, *Confessions of an Igloo Dweller*, p. 267; the print he refers to is also documented in Blodgett, *Kenojuak*, p. 80 (Fig. 1); in Eber, *In Cape Dorset We Do It This Way*, p.24; and in Hoffmann, *Im Schatten der Sonne – Zeitgenössische Kunst der Indianer und Eskimos in Kanada*, p. 537.

[28] The 1990 collection, for example, contained only two prints, each depicting a wolf.

[29] Blodgett, *Kenojuak*, p.35.

[30] ibid, p. 37.

[31] James Houston, *Arts of the Eskimo: Prints*, Introduction, p. 7; Montreal 1974 and Barry Press 1967.

[32] The snowmobiles are mostly called 'skidoos,' even when they are not actually of that make, but Polaris or Yamaha snowmobiles instead. Joseph-Armand Bombardier built the first snowmobile in 1922 and called it a 'ski dog'; a typo-

graphical error resulted in 'skidoo.'

33 The ATV (All Traction Vehicle, or All-Terrain Vehicle) is usually a four-wheeled scooter with four-wheel drive, and commonplace throughout the Arctic regions. Normal scooters were introduced to Cape Dorset in the 1960s and were soon followed by motorized tricycles; their proneness to accidents led to the introduction of four-wheel ATVs.

34 The film won the British Academy Award 'Best Film' in 1964-65.

35 Until recently, the house was inhabited by Kiugak [Kiawak] Ashoona, the well-known artist.

36 Her full name is Kenojuak Udluriaq Amaru Siaja Ashevak – Amaru was her great-grandmother, the mother of Alariaq; Udluriaq was her father's sister, and Siaja is her Christian name.

37 When the Inuit refer to the 'old days' they mean the time before they moved into solid houses in the settlements.

38 The 'old way of life' is the way the Inuit people lived before moving from the camps to the settlements.

39 See the report by Peter Pitseolak in *People from Our Side*, p. 40 ff..

40 In Germany, the 'Inuit Galerie Mannheim' has been endeavouring for many years to make Inuit art known to a wider audience. As well works by Kenojuak can be obtained through the gallery.

41 Blodgett, *Kenojuak*, p. 74.

42 From the catalogue *1993 Cape Dorset – Annual Graphics Collection*.

Kenojuak's family tree

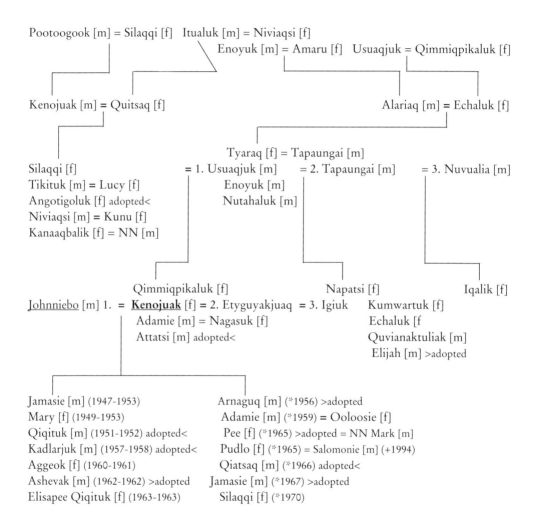

Pootoogook [m] = Silaqqi [f]   Itualuk [m] = Niviaqsi [f]

Enoyuk [m] = Amaru [f]   Usuaqjuk = Qimmiqpikaluk [f]

Kenojuak [m] = Quitsaq [f]

Alariaq [m] = Echaluk [f]

Tyaraq [f] = Tapaungai [m]

Silaqqi [f]
Tikituk [m] = Lucy [f]
Angotigoluk [f] adopted<
Niviaqsi [m] = Kunu [f]
Kanaaqbalik [f] = NN [m]

= 1. Usuaqjuk [m]
Enoyuk [m]
Nutahaluk [m]

= 2. Tapaungai [m]

= 3. Nuvualia [m]

Qimmiqpikaluk [f]

Napatsi [f]

Iqalik [f]

Johnniebo [m] 1. = **Kenojuak** [f] = 2. Etyguyakjuaq = 3. Igiuk   Kumwartuk [f]
Adamie [m] = Nagasuk [f]   Echaluk [f
Attatsi [m] adopted<   Quvianaktuliak [m]
                                                               Elijah [m] >adopted

Jamasie [m] (1947-1953)   Arnaguq [m] (*1956) >adopted
Mary [f] (1949-1953)   Adamie [m] (*1959) = Ooloosie [f]
Qiqituk [m] (1951-1952) adopted<   Pee [f] (*1965) >adopted = NN Mark [m]
Kadlarjuk [m] (1957-1958) adopted<   Pudlo [f] (*1965) = Salomonie [m] (+1994)
Aggeok [f] (1960-1961)   Qiatsaq [m] (*1966) adopted<
Ashevak [m] (1962-1962) >adopted   Jamasie [m] (*1967) >adopted
Elisapee Qiqituk [f] (1963-1963)   Silaqqi [f] (*1970)

218

Johnniebo's family tree

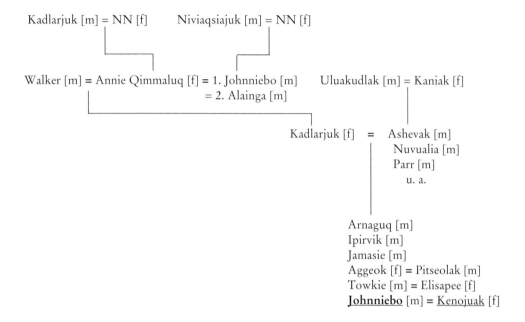

Symbols:

= ~ married
= ~ partnership without marriage
>adopted ~ adopted from other parents
adopted< ~ given to other parents for adoption

Chronology

1927	Kenojuak's birth in Camp Ikirasak (beginning of January; official date of birth, however, is 3 October)
1928	Birth of her brother Adamie; move to Pujjunnaq [Mansel Island]
1931	Murder of Kenojuak's father Usuaqjuk (winter 1930/31); return to Sikusiilaq and Camp Sapujjuaq – Kenojuak lives here (with interruptions) with her grandmother Quitsaq until 1946
1935	Marriage of her mother, Silaqqi, to Tapaungai
1937-1946	Temporary stays in Camp Igalaalik with her mother
1946	Death of Silaqqi's 2nd husband Tapaungai; marriage of Kenojuak to Johnniebo in the summer (church wedding in winter 1948/49); short stay in a camp on Saqbak Bay; move to Peter Pitseolak's Camp Kiattuuq
1947	Average of the supply ship *Nascopie* (21 July); marriage of Kenojuak's mother Silaqqi to Nuvualia; birth of Kenojuak's son Jamasie (1st child)

1948	Death of Kenojuak's grandmother Quitsaq
1949	Move to Camp Saatturittuq; birth of Kenojuak's daughter Mary (2nd child)
1950	Setting up of school and nursing station in Cape Dorset
1951	Arrival of James and Alma Houston in Cape Dorset; Johnniebo and Kenojuak move to Camp Qarmaaqjuk; birth von Kenojuak's son Qiqituk (3rd child), given for adoption to Latchaolassie and Saimaijuk Akesuk (the child died in 1952)
1952-1955	Kenojuak's stay in a tuberculosis hospital in Quebec City
1953	Death von Kenojuak's children Jamasie and Mary; building of an Anglican church under the leadership of the 'Eskimo King,' Pootoogook
1955	Kenojuak's return to Sikusiilaq (Camp Kangiaq); starting craft work with Alma Houston
1956	Birth of Arnaguq (24 November) as son of Aggeak and Sheorak Petaulassie, adopted by Johnniebo and Kenojuak

1957	Beginning of print making in Cape Dorset; death of Johnniebo's mother Kadlarjuk; return to Peter Pitseolak's Camp Kiattuuq; birth of a son, Kadlarjuk, given to Abraham and Etyguyakjuaq Etungat for adoption (the child died in 1958)
1958	Kenojuak's first print, 'Rabbit Eating Seaweed'
1959	Birth of her son Adamie (24 July); Kenojuak's first drawings on paper
1960	Move to Camp Itilliaqjuk; arrival of Terry Ryan (James Houston's successor)
1961	Birth of her daughter Aggeok, who died soon after; Alma Houston leaves Cape Dorset with her children
1962	Adoption of a boy, Ashevak, from his mother Nee Itulu, but the child dies a few months later; James Houston leaves Cape Dorset; film recording for 'Eskimo Artist – Kenojuak'; first copper engravings by Kenojuak and Johnniebo
1963	Birth of her daughter Elisapee Qiqituk, who died the following day

1965	Birth of Pee (19 February) as daughter of Ijitsiaq [Eegeetsiak] and Nitani Peter, adopted by Johnniebo and Kenojuak; birth of her own daughter Pudlo (11 October)
1966	Johnniebo and Kenojuak's move to Cape Dorset; birth of their son Qiatsaq (27 December), given to Aggeak and Timangiak Petaulassie for adoption
1967	Birth of Jamasie (4 May) as son of Aggeak and Timangiak Petaulassie, adopted by Johnniebo and Kenojuak; conferral of the 'Order of Canada' to Kenojuak in Ottawa (24 November)
1969	Co-working of Kenojuak and Johnniebo in Ottawa on a mural relief for the Canadian Pavilion at Expo '70 in Osaka
1970	Birth of her daughter Silaqqi (24 January); journey to Osaka; Johnniebo and Kenojuak choose Ashevak as their surname; Kenojuak's print 'The Enchanted Owl' from 1960 is taken for a 6-cent postage stamp to mark 100 years of the Northwest Territories
1971	First journey to Halifax with Johnniebo; abandonment of the last permanent camps in the Sikusiilaq region

1972	Death of Johnniebo (8 September)
1973	Partnership between Kenojuak and Etyguyakjuak Pee
1974	Election to the Royal Canadian Academy of Arts; 2nd journey to Halifax
1976	Meeting with Jessie Oonark in Ottawa (guest at the Canadian Conference of Catholic Bishops)
1977	Death of Etyguyakjuak Pee (21 June); journey to the World Wildlife Fund in Toronto with Kananginak Pootoogook
1979	Partnership between Kenojuak and Igiuk Joannassie; several families from Cape Dorset try to return to camps for the whole year
1980	Journey to Rotterdam (the Netherlands) to the opening of the exhibition entitled 'The Inuit Print'; Kenojuak's print 'The Return of the Sun' from 1961 is the motif on a 17-cent postage stamp issued in the Canadian Post Office's set of Inuit stamps
1981	Death of Igiuk Joanassie

1982	Awarded the 'Companion to the Order of Canada'
1990	Death of her brother, Adamie Alariaq
1991	Honorary Doctorate awarded by Queen's University, Kingston
1992	Honorary Doctorate awarded by the Law Faculty of the University of Toronto
1993	Kenojuak's print 'The Owl' from 1969 is used on an 86-cent postage stamp in the 'Art Canada' series
1994	Loss of her grandson Uqittuq (son of her daughter Pudlo)
1995	Conferral of 'National Aboriginal Achievement Award' (Lifetime Achievement) in Vancouver
1996	Journey to Ottawa, the first journey she undertakes on her own and pays for herself
1999	Edition of a 25-cent coin bearing an owl motif by Kenojuak on the occasion of Nunavut's inauguration

Index of persons

Note: The spelling of names is based on the syllabic and phonetic rendering by the Inuit themselves; names that are particularly well known in English influenced spelling are provided in square brackets. * means year of birth.

Adamie: see under *Alariaq, Adamie* and *Ashevak, Adamie*

Adla, Kalai (*1927): artist well known for his carvings; was married to the artist Tye Adla (1936-1990), a sister of Iyola Kingwatsiak

Aggeok: see under *Pitseolak, Aggeok*

Ainalik, Quaraq: a sister of Qalingo's, related to Kenojuak's grandmother Quitsaq; lives in Ivujivik (North Quebec)

Akesuk, Latchaolassie (*1919): husband of Kenojuak's cousin Saimaijuk; adoptive father of Kenojuak's 3rd child, Qiqituk (1951-1952); stone carver with a very personal style; in 1970, won 2nd prize in the Sculpture Competition in Yellowknife organised by the Canadian Eskimo Arts Council

Akesuk, Tuqlik (1887-1965): well-known carver of stone sculptures; father of Latchaolassie Akesuk and the artist Nicotai Mills (*1942), who has earned distinction in recent years with her excellent prints

Alariaq (....-1952): Kenojuak's paternal grandfather; a shaman prior to Christianisation

Alariaq, Adamie (1928-1990): a brother of Kenojuak's; married to Nakasuk

Alariaq, Timmun (*1954): son of Adamie Alariaq, married to Kristiina (*1954)

Annie Qimmaluq (~1850-....): grandmother of Johnniebo Ashevak

Aoudla: see under *Pee, Aoudla*

Applewhite, A. F. 'Bill': worked from 1950-1952 as a teacher in Cape Dorset, his wife Phyllis as a nurse

Arnakotak: see under *Houston, Alma*

Ashevak (....-....): father of Johnniebo; brother of Nuvualia and Parr; married to Kadlarjuk; see also *Kadlarjuk*

Ashevak, Adamie (*1959): son of Kenojuak, married to Ooloosie; becoming increasingly well known for his stone sculptures

Ashevak, Arnaguq (*1956): adopted son of Kenojuak (natural parents: Aggeak and Sheorak Petaulassie); an artist gaining increasing recognition for his prints

Ashevak, Johnniebo (1923-1972): husband of Kenojuak; artist in stone carving and drawing

Ashevak, Qinnuajuak [Kenojuak] (*1927): daughter of Usuaqjuk and Silaqqi

Ashevak, Towkie (1912-....): a brother of Johnniebo's; married to Elisapee (+1959)

Ashoona (....-1945): husband of Pitseolak Ashoona, brother of Tapaungai; outstanding hunter

Ashoona, Kiugak [Kiawak] (*1933): son of Pitseolak Ashoona and brother of Qaqaq Ashoona; well-known artist

Ashoona, Mayoreak (*1946): daughter of Sheorak Petaulassie (and half-sister of Kenojuak's adopted son Arnaguq); was married to Qaqaq Ashoona and has made a name for herself with stone sculptures and above all with her prints

Ashoona, Pitseolak (1904-1983): had 17 children, of whom 11 died young; one of the most important Inuit woman artists; honours include membership of the Royal Canadian Academy; received 'Order of Canada' in 1977; in 1971, her book *Pitseolak: Pictures out of my life* was made into a film by the National Film Board (NFB) of Canada

Ashoona, Qaqaq (1928-1996): the eldest son of Pitseolak Ashoona and one of the leading stone carvers in Cape Dorset; also an excellent hunter; moved permanently to Camp Saatturittuq with his wife, Mayoreak

Ashoona, Sorosilutu (*1941): wife of Kiugak [Kiawak] Ashoona; well-known for her drawings and prints

Attatsi [Attachie] (*1931): a brother of Kenojuak's, the 4th child of Usuaqjuk and Silaqqi

Conrad, Felix (....-1946): Manager of the Baffin Trading Company, Cape Dorset trading post

Eleeshushe (1896-1975): half-sister of Pootoogook and Peter Pitseolak; 2nd wife of Parr; represented in several Cape Dorset print collections; produced more than 1,000 drawings

Enoyuk (....-1930): a son of Alariaq's; younger brother of Kenojuak's father Usuaqjuk

Etidlooie, Etidlooie (1910-1981): first marriage to Kadlarjuk [Kulluaqjuk] (....-1960), then second marriage to the woman artist Kingmeata Etidlooie (1915-1989)

Etidlooie, Sheojuk (1929-1999): wife of Pauta Saila's deceased brother Etidlooie; achieved distinction in recent years with very impressive drawings (prints)

Etungat, Abraham (*1911): married to Etyguyakjuaq; began making sculptures in 1961, including sculptures in bronze

Ezekiel, Ashevak (*1932): natural son of Aggeok Pitseolak, the sister of Johnniebo Ashevak and second wife of Peter Pitseolak; stone carver; married to the artist Mary Ashevak Ezekiel (*1932)

Houston, Alma [Allie] – *Arnakotak, the tall-grown lady*: first wife of James Houston; tended primarily to the craft work done by the women

Houston, James – *'Saumik, the left-handed one'* (*1921): worked in Cape Dorset from 1951-1962 as artistic adviser to the Inuit; established the West Baffin Eskimo Co-operative with his first wife Alma [Allie]; his second wife's name is Alice

Igyvadluk: see under *Pootoogook, Igyvadluk*

Ikummiaq [Ekoomiak], Sarah: interpreter on board the *C. D. Howe*, a friend of Kenojuak's since her journey home from her hospital stay in Quebec; was involved in translating the Inuktitut text of 'Pitseolak: Pictures out of my life'

Ipeelee, Osuitok [Oshweetok] (*1922): was married to the artist Nipisa Osuitok (1925-1980); an artist who is constantly seeking new paths in his art and his methods of work; was the first, for example, to install his own power generator in order to be independent of the public power grid; lives today in a house suitable for someone his age; continues to produce superb sculptures, despite losing his strength, and can be seen almost daily in the Co-op art centre

Iqalik: see under *Pootoogook, Iqalik*

Itulu, Nee (....-1991): originally from Iqaluit, mother of the boy Ashevak who was adopted by Johnniebo and Kenojuak in 1962 and died soon after

Iyola: see under *Kingwatsiak, Iyola*

Jaku (....-1923): originally Mamirajak, then dubbed Kigak ('the messenger'); buried since 1982 near Camp Itilliaqjuq

Joanassie, Igiuk [Egeyuk] (1923-1981): stone carver; Kenojuak's partner from 1979 until his death

Johnniebo: see under *Ashevak, Johnniebo*

Kadlarjuk (....-....): great-grandfather of Johnniebo Ashevak

Kadlarjuk (~1874-1957): mother of Johnniebo; had six children by his father, Ashevak: precise dates are missing regarding the three elder sons Arnaguq, Ipirvik and Jamasie; the only daughter, Aggeok, was born in 1906 (she was the second wife of Peter Pitseolak); two more sons then followed: Towkie in 1912 and Johnniebo in 1923

Kalai: see under *Adla, Kalai*

Kananginak: see under *Pootoogook, Kananginak*

Kanaaqbalik (....-1969): a younger sister of Kenojuak's mother Silaqqi

Kavavau: see under *Manumie, Qavavau*

Kenojuak: see under *Ashevak, Qinnuajuak [Kenojuak]*

Kingwatsiak (....-....): father of Iyola Kingwatsiak and Tye Adla, among others; went as a mere 16-year-old on a whaling ship to England, where he lived for approx. two years; he died, more than 80 years of age, when his polystyrene igloo caught fire

Kingwatsiak, Iyola (*1933): son of Kingwatsiak; a recognized stone carver and print artist

Kopapik: see under *Qaqjurajuk, Kopapik* and *Quppapik, Simeonie*

Kudjuakjuk: see under *Qaqjurajuk, Mary*

Kunu (1923-1966): wife of Kenojuak's uncle Niviaqsi; mother of the artists Qiatsuq Niviaqsi and Pitseolak Niviaqsi; in 1959, one of the first Inuit women involved in the annual print collection of the West Baffin Eskimo Co-operative

Kuyu, the 'Girl Friday' at the nursing station: probably Kuyu Uttuqi [Ottokie] (*1931), the second daughter of Peter Pitseolak from his first marriage to Annie; married to Quvianaqtuliaq Uttuqi

Latchaolassie: see under *Akesuk, Latchaolassie*

Lucy: see under *Qinnuayuak, Lucy*

Lukta: see under *Qiatsuq, Lukta*

Manning, Jeannie (*1958): daughter of Tommy and Udluriak Manning; Inuktitut interpreter (among other things)

Manning, Jimmy Tigugligak (*1951): natural son of George Pitseolak; adopted son of Tommy Manning; Assistant General Manager of the West Baffin Eskimo Co-operative; married to Pitseolala since 1996

Manning, Pitseolala (*1966): daughter of Nutsalia and Kumwartuq Mathewsie (Kumwartuq: daughter of Kenojuak's mother Silaqqi from her second marriage to Tapaungai)

Manning, Tommy (1927-1994): manager at the Hudson's Bay Company; husband of Peter Pitseolak's eldest daughter Udluriak; father of, among others, Jeannie Manning, and the adoptive father of Jimmy Manning

Manning, Udluriak (1924-1971): eldest daughter of Peter Pitseolak (from his first marriage with Annie); wife of Tommy Manning; mother of, among others, Jeannie Manning; only briefly active as an artist

Manumie, Qavavau [Mannomee, Kavavaow] (*1958): son of the artist Davidee Manumie; brother of the artists Tukiki Manumie and Aqjangajuk Shaa; gifted up-coming artist; works as printer in the Co-op

Mark, Pee (*1965): daughter of Ijitsiaq and Nitani Peter; adopted by Johnniebo and Kenojuak; lives with four children in Ivujivik; her eldest son Siyuktuk adopted by her natural parents, and her youngest child by her natural brother Kuyu Peter

Napatsi [Napachie]: see under *Pootoogook, Napatsi*

Natsivak (1919-1962): married to Nu Pudlalik; mother of the woman artist Papiarak Tuqiqi (*1941); created graphic prints (some of which were included in the annual collections for 1960 and 1961)

Ningeukaluk (....-....): was first married to Parr, then became the wife of Pootoogook through exchange of wives

Niviaqsi [Niviaksiak] (1908-1959): a brother of Kenojuak's mother Silaqqi; one of the first graphic artists in Cape Dorset, acknowledged for his talent to draw and to carve in stone; husband of the artist Kunu and father of the well-known artists Qiatsuq Niviaqsi (*1941) and Pitseolak Niviaqsi (*1947)

Nutahaluk (*1929): the youngest son of Alariaq (Kenojuak's uncle); lives in Iqaluit

Nuvualia (....-1955): a brother of Johnniebo's father Ashevak and of Parr; 3rd husband of Silaqqi; from this marriage was born a daughter, Iqalik (*1949), who is married to Elijah Pootoogook

Okpik, Abraham 'Abe' (1929-1997), a well-known Inuit leader, was the first Inuk in the Northwest Territories Territorial Council, the precursor to the Northwest Territories Legislative Assembly

Oonark, Jessie (1906-1985): major woman graphic artist from the community of Baker Lake

Oqutaq, Qimmikpikaluk (*~ 1924): elder sister of Kenojuak

Osuitok: see under *Ipeelee, Osuitok*

Parr (1893-1969): a brother of Johnniebo's father Ashevak; did not begin drawing until an elderly man in 1961; in the eight years to his death, he produced more than 2,000 drawings featuring traditional daily life in the Arctic; he and his second wife Eleeshushe had nine children, including Quvianaqtuliaq (*1930) and Nuna (*1949), both of whom are renowned artists (Nuna is the youngest natural son of Parr's daughter Tayaraq, who died young, i.e. his natural grandson, and was adopted by Parr)

Peck, Edmund James – '*Okhamuk, who speaks so well*' (1850-....): Anglican missionary who exerted a major influence on the Inuit; introduced the system of syllabic writing among the Inuit from 1876 onwards

Pee, Aoudla (1920-1988): brother of Etyguyakjuaq Pee, Kenojuak's partner for a period; was previously a well-known camp leader; created some remarkable stone sculptures

Pee, Etyguyakjuaq (....-1977): Kenojuak's partner from 1973 until his death

Petaulassie, Aggeak (1922-1983): well-known stone carver; father of the similarly well-known stone carvers Etidlooie Petaulassie (*1944), Qatsiyak Petaulassie (*1948) and Pavinaq Petaulassie (*1961) and of Kenojuak's adopted son Arnaguq

Petaulassie, Sheorak (1923-1961): first wife of Aggeak; mother of the artist Mayoreak Ashoona and of Ken ojuak's adopted son Arnaguq; known for her print work (e.g. the logo of the West Baffin Eskimo Co-operative was her work)

Petaulassie, Timangiak (*1940): second wife of Aggeak; mother of Kenojuak's adopted son Jamasie; was active as an artist in the 1960s; is now a well-known throat singer

Peter, Ijitsiaq [Eegeetsiak] (*1937): married to Nitani, a daughter of Iqaluk Goo's; father of Kenojuak's adopted daughter Pee; known for his stone sculptures; in 1970, won first prize in Yellowknife at the Sculpture Competition organised by the Canadian Eskimo Arts Council

Pfeiffer, Harold (1908-1997): sculptor in Quebec

Pfeiffer, Walter: Harold Pfeiffer's brother; the doctor responsible for Kenojuak's medical treatment in the Quebec hospital

Pitseolak: see under *Ashoona, Pitseolak* and *Pitseolak, Peter*

Pitseolak, Aggeok (1906-1977): only sister of Johnniebo Ashevak and the second wife of Peter Pitseolak; mother of the artist Mary Pitseolak (*1931)

Pitseolak, Peter (1902-1973): important camp leader; brother of Pootoogook, grandfather of Jeannie Manning; married first to Annie (+1941), then to Aggeok (sister of Johnniebo Ashevak); began to paint watercolours in the late 1930s, and since 1942 had been an active photographer; became well known through his prints in the 1970-1975 annual collections of the West Baffin Eskimo Co-operative, also through his book, co-authored with Dorothy H. Eber, entitled *People from Our Side*, in which he describes for his descendants his experience of living in and between two cultures (published posthumously in 1975)

Pitseolala: see under *Manning, Pitseolala*

Pootoogook – 'Big Toe' (1887-1959) (not to be confused with Kenojuak's great-grandfather): brother of Peter Pitseolak; unusually powerful Inuit leader, referred to throughout the South Baffin region as the 'Eskimo King' on account of his considerable influence; lived for a long time in Camp Ikirasak, then moved for health reasons to the Cape Dorset settlement in the late 1950s, where he began to draw; his prints were included in the 1959 and 1961 annual collections

Pootoogook, Elijah (*1943): a natural son of Etidlooie Etidlooie, adopted by Pudlat Pootoogook (*1919); married to Kenojuak's half-sister Iqalik; was involved in various annual collections of the West Baffin Eskimo Co-operative and in constructing the Canadian pavilion at Expo '70 in Osaka

Pootoogook, Igyvadluk [Eegyvudluk] (*1931): a son of Pootoogook's and married to the artist Napatsi Pootoogook, the only daughter of Pitseolak Ashoona

Pootoogook, Iqalik (*1949): daughter born of the marriage between Kenojuak's mother Silaqqi and Nuvualia; a stone carver

Pootoogook, Kananginak (*1935): the youngest son of Pootoogook and, like his father, a very strong personality; internationally renowned as both a sculptor and graphic artist

Pootoogook, Napatsi [Napatchie] (*1938): the only daughter of Pitseolak Ashoona still alive; married to Pootoogook's son Igyvadluk Pootoogook and the mother of the well-known stone carver: see Pootoogook (*1967); known not only for her prints but also for her paintings with acrylics

Pootoogook, Paulassie (*1927): the eldest son of the Inuit leader Pootoogook, married to Josie; talented stone carver; father of the artist Tukikikuluk Pootoogook (*1943)

Pootoogook, Salamonie (....-1955): fellow patient of Kenojuak's; died in a lung sanatorium in Hamilton (Ontario)

Pudlat, Mary (*1923): second wife of Samuellie Pudlat, sister-in-law of Pudlo Pudlat; she is well-known for her drawings and her graphics have been included in many annual collections; she created the wall hanging in the Iqaluit Visitor's Centre

Pudlat, Padluq [Pudlo] (1916-1993): famous graphic artist

Pudlo (*1965): daughter of Johnniebo and Kenojuak; was married to Salomonie (+1994); lives in Salluit, her 2 daughters live with Kenojuak

Qalingo (....-....): important personage on Mansel Island (Pujjunnaq)

Qaqjurajuk [Qayuryuk], Kopapik 'A' (1923-1969): well-known stone carver; step-father of the well-known graphic artist and throat-singer Qaunaq Mikkigak (*1932)

Qaqjurajuk [Kudjuakjuk], Mary (1908-1982): fellow patient of Kenojuak's in Quebec; carved stone sculptures and designed prints that were included in several annual collections of the West Baffin Eskimo Co-operative; the children from her first marriage include her son Laisa (married to Tikituk and Lucy Qinnuayuak's daughter Arnasuk) and her daughter Qaunaq Mikkigak (*1932), also a well-known artist; second marriage to Kopapik 'A' Qaqjurajuk

Quaraq: see under *Ainalik, Quaraq*

Qiatsuq [Kiatshuk] (1888-1966): originally a shaman, later professed the Christian faith; prominent carver and graphic artist

Qiatsuq, Lukta (*1928): a son of Qiatsuq's [Kiatshuk]; husband of Pudlo, the daughter of Johnniebo Ashevak's brother Towkie; father of the artists Pootoogook Qiatsuq (*1959), Qiatsuq Qiatsuq (*1962) and Padlaya Qiatsuq (*1965)

Qimmikpikaluk: see under *Oqutaq, Qimmikpikaluk*

Qimuakjuk [Johnniebo] (....-1888): adoptive father of Johnniebo Ashevak's mother Kadlarjuk

Qinnuayuak, Lucy (1915-1982): step-daughter of Quitsaq's brother Tagatuk; wife of Silaqqi's brother Tikituk; very well-known for her drawings and graphic art

Qinnuayuak, Tikituk (1908-1992): a brother of Kenojuak's mother Silaqqi; husband of Lucy Qinnuayuak; a stone carver and printer

Quitsaq [Kooweesa] (....-1948): Kenojuak's maternal grandmother (the mother of Silaqqi)

Quppapik [Kopapik], Simeonie (1909 -1993): brother of the famous graphic artist Pudlo Pudlat; his own work has often been included in the annual collections of the West Baffin Eskimo Co-operative

Ryan, Terry (*1933): following his studies at the Ontario College of Art he has been in Cape Dorset since 1960; General Manager of the West Baffin Eskimo Co-op Art Centre since 1961 (as successor to James Houston); first wife Patricia, second wife Leslie Boyd

Saggiak (1897 – 1980): camp leader in Itilliaqjuk for a time; known for his stone carvings

Saila, Pauta (*1916): son of a shaman and nephew of Peter Pitseolak; one of Cape Dorset's most renowned sculpture carvers; first marriage to Matsauzaq, second to the well-known artist Pitaloosie Saila (*1942)

Saumik: see under _Houston, James_

Silaqqi [Seelaki; officially: Silaqqi Ashevak] (1902-1985): mother of Kenojuak; first marriage was to Usuaqjuk (- 1931), the second to Tapaungai (- 1946), and the third to Nuvualia (1947-1955)

Soper, J. Dewey (1893-1982): natural scientist and artist; undertook four Arctic expeditions between 1923 and 1931

Takatuk (....-....): brother of Kenojuak's grandmother Quitsaq

Tapaungai (....-1946): first marriage to Kenojuak's aunt Tayaraq, then second marriage to Kenojuak's mother Silaqqi; five children were born of this second marriage: Napatsi, the eldest daughter, lives today in Kimmirut (Lake Harbour); Kumwartuq Mathewsie, the 2nd daughter, was born in 1941, moved back to Cape Dorset from Iqaluit in the early 1970s (following the death of her first husband Nutsalia by whom she had the daughter Pitseolala Manning), was then living with the stone printer Pee Mikkigak (1940-1996); Quvianaqtuliaq Tapaungai (*1942), married to Towkie's daughter Neevee (i.e. a niece of Johnniebo Ashevak), lives and works as an artist in Cape Dorset; the 3rd daughter, Iqaluk [Echalook], moved to Iqaluit; Elijah, the 5th child, was given up for adoption

Tayaraq (....-1935): eldest sister of Kenojuak's father Usuaqjuk (an aunt of Kenojuak)

Tikituk: see under *Qinnuayuak, Tikituk*

Towkie: see under *Ashevak, Towkie*

Udluriak: see under *Manning, Udluriak*

Usuaqjuk (~1900-1931): son of Alariaq; first husband of Silaqqi and father of Kenojuak

Walker: natural father of Johnniebo Ashevak's mother Kadlarjuk; captain of a whaling ship

Names of the Sikusiilaq camps

Note: In general, there is considerable variation in the way that names and place names are spelt. As a basic principle throughout this book, the syllabic, phonetic version used by the Inuit is applied; in order to provide some basic orientation, a listing is provided of some synonyms that result from the influence of English. The numbers in square brackets refer to the position of the camps in the map on the next page (according to information given by Timmun Alariaq and Jimmy Manning).

Igalaalik – Egalalik, Igalallik [4]
Ikirasak – Ikerrasak, Ikirashaq, Ikirassak [8]
Iqalurajuk [7]
Itilliaqjuk – Etidliajuk, Etilliakjuk, Ittiliakjuk [3]
Kallusiqbik – Kalosebek, Kadlooshukbik, Kadlusukbik, Katlusivik [10]
Kangiaq – Kangeak, Kangiyak, Kungia [6]
Kiattuuq – Keakto, Keatuk [1]
Qarmaaqjuk – Amadjuak [Bay], Kamadjuak, Qarmaajuk [11]
Saatturittuq – Sartowitok, Satoretok, Shartowitok, Shatureetuk [2]
Sapujjuaq – Shapujuak, Shupujuak [5]
Saqbak – Shukbuk [Bay], Sukbuk [Bay] [9]

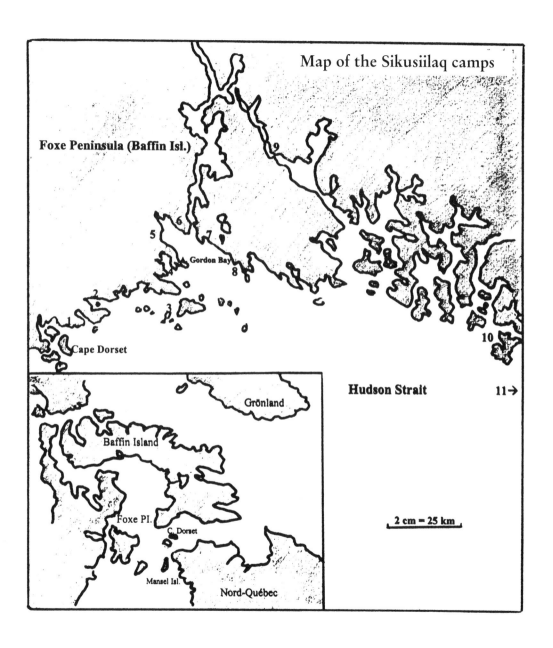

Map of the Sikusiilaq camps

Foxe Peninsula (Baffin Isl.)

Gordon Bay

Cape Dorset

Hudson Strait 11→

Grönland

Baffin Island

Foxe Pl.

C. Dorset

Mansel Isl.

Nord-Québec

2 cm = 25 km

Frequently used Inuktitut words

Note: The spelling used for the words occurring in the book and listed below is based on the syllabic, phonetic version of the Sikusiilarmiut, and on Lucien Schneider, 'Ulirnaisigutiit, an Inuktitut-English Dictionary of Northern Quebec, Labrador and Eastern Arctic Dialects'; Quebec 1985.

aglu = breathing hole for seals
amautiq = women's parka with a hood, also for carrying small children
angakkuq = shaman
iglu (igloo) = snow house
Inuk, *pl.* Inuit = human being ('a being with a soul')
inuksuk, *pl.* inuksuit = stone figure ('like an Inuk')
Inuktitut = the language of the Inuit
kamik = boots (usually fur boots)
maktaaq = whale skin with the blubber below
natsiq = seal
Nunavut = land of the Inuit ('our land')
qallunaaq, *pl.* qallunaat = non-Inuk ('human with eyebrows')
qajaq = kayak (a one-seater boat)
qamutik = sled
qarmaq = sod house
qulliq = stone lamp used by the Inuit
Sikusiilaq = 'where there is no ice', 'where the water does not freeze'
Sikusiilarmiut = people from Sikusiilaq
ulu = woman's knife (semi-circular knife)
umiaq = family boat (for up to 20 people)

Bibliography

The following literature helped us prepare for the interviews with Kenojuak and served as an additional source of information in general:

Applewhite, A. F. 'Bill' in Macpherson, Norman John, *Dreams and Visions – Education in the Northwest Territories From Early Days to 1984*, pp. 71-74, Government of the Northwest Territories, Canada; Department of Education, Yellowknife 1991

Blodgett, Jean, *Kenojuak*, The Mintmark Press, Firefly Books, Toronto 1985

Blodgett, Jean & Gustavison, Susan (Eds.), *Strange Scenes, Early Cape Dorset Drawings*, The McMichael Canadian Art Collection, Kleinburg 1993

Blodgett, Jean (Ed.), *In Cape Dorset We Do It This Way*, The McMichael Canadian Art Collection, Kleinburg 1991

Eber, Dorothy H. (Ed.), *Pitseolak: Pictures out of my life*, University of Washington Press, Seattle 1971

Eber, Dorothy H., *When the Whalers Were Up North*, McGill-Queen's University Press, Montréal 1989

Hoffmann, Gerhard (Ed.), *Im Schatten der Sonne – Zeitgenössische Kunst der Indianer and Eskimos in Kanada* [In the Shadow of the Sun – Contemporary Art of the Indians and Eskimos in Canada], Edition Cantz, Stuttgart 1988 & Canadian Museum of Civilization, Ottawa 1988

Houston, James, *Confessions of an Igloo Dweller*, McClelland & Stewart, Toronto 1995

Leroux, Odette et al. (Eds.), *Inuit Women Artists*, Canadian Museum of Civilization, Ottawa 1994

Pitseolak, Peter & Eber, Dorothy H., *People from Our Side*, Hurtig Publishers, Edmonton 1975 & McGill-Queen's University Press, Montreal 1993

Note on the photographs:

There is a wide range of literature in English on Kenojuak's art, containing pictures of her work up to the late 1980s. As far as pictorial material is concerned, this biography seeks only to add to what is already available, and above all to provide some insight into the artist's everyday life today and the environment in which she lives. For that reason, only photographs and reprints of Kenojuak's work from the 1990s are published here.

We are especially grateful to:

- Kenojuak Ashevak – for the enormous trust she demonstrated towards us by telling us about her life in the course of many interviews in summer 1996 and spring 1997;
- Jeannie Manning – for her invaluable assistance as a sensitive interpreter;
- Jimmy Manning – who paved our way for preparing and carrying through our interviews as well as for obtaining additional information, and for finding literature and picture material;
- Leslie Boyd – for advice and support in obtaining copyright for works by Kenojuak;
- Timmun Alariaq, Kenojuak's nephew, and his wife Kristiina – for letting us have their beach house in Cape Dorset to carry out our work and who also gave us the opportunity to become familiar with places where Kenojuak used to live 'on the land';
- Barbara Fohrer and Karin Richter-Oldekop – for their tireless assistance in proof-reading.

In addition, we would like to express our gratitude to the following persons and institutions for having given us kind permission to quote important, informative parts from their publications.

- Jean Blodgett c/o The McMichael Canadian Art Collection, Kleinburg, ON, regarding Blodgett, *Kenojuak*
- Leslie Boyd c/o Dorset Fine Arts, Toronto, ON, regarding *Cape Dorset Annual Graphics Collection 1979* and *1993*

- Pat Fehely c/o Feheley Fine Arts, Toronto, ON, regarding *Cape Dorset Annual Graphics Collection 1977*
- Government of the Northwest Territories of Canada, Department of Education, Culture, and Employment, Yellowknife, NW, regarding Macpherson, *Dreams and Visions*
- McClelland & Stewart, Toronto, ON, and James Houston, regarding Houston, *Confessions of an Igloo Dweller*, and Houston, *Art of the Eskimo: Prints*
- McGill-Queen's University Press, Montréal, QC, and Dorothy H. Eber, regarding Peter Pitseolak, *People from Our Side*

About the author

Ansgar Walk (born 1929) studied natural sciences and, in addition, philosophy and literature. He is interested not only in scientific aspects regarding the Arctic, but also in issues concerning the social development and the art of the Inuit. He and his wife have thus been frequent visitors to the Canadian Northeast in recent years. Several journeys to Cape Dorset (on Baffin Island) brought him into close contact with the artists who live there, this book being one of the results. Other books about the Arctic by Ansgar Walk and published by Pendragon Verlag, Bielefeld, are: *Im Land der Inuit – Arktisches Tagebuch [In the Land of the Inuit – Arctic Diary]* and *Der Polarbär kam spät abends – Skizzen von der Wager Bay [The Polar Bear Came Late at Night – Sketches of Wager Bay]*.